sesame, soy, spice

90 ASIAN-ISH VEGAN AND GLUTEN-FREE RECIPES
TO RECONNECT, ROOT, AND RESTORE

Remy Morimoto Park

WM
WILLIAM MORROW
An Imprint of HarperCollinsPublishers

For my family,
both blood and chosen,
who have taste tested
a million iterations of
every recipe in this book
and tried their very best
to transcribe our family
recipes so that I could
share them with you.

contents

introduction

I was a picky buttered-pasta, no-parsley, no-black-pepper kid born to a half-Japanese, half-Taiwanese mother who is a lover of foie gras, fine cheeses, and wine (just not natural wine, which apparently doesn't taste as good, even if might be better for you) and a Korean father who is a passionate advocate for white, short-grain rice served alongside every meal. They named me Remy, after Rémy Martin, the cognac they enjoyed on their first date, which is always a fun story to tell, especially because I got sober more than seven years ago.

Growing up, there was always an abundance of food on the table at our house and all of my relatives' homes. We greeted one another by asking "Have you eaten?" in lieu of "How are you?," and nearly all our family meetups revolved around food—whether we were eating at a new restaurant, celebrating a holiday, or sitting around the round table, shelling pistachios and sharing life updates. Both my uncles, Eugene and Raba, were restaurateurs in Manhattan, my mum befriended many restaurateurs and eventually became involved with a friend's restaurant in Shanghai, and my maternal grandmother could whip up a meal for six even when the fridge was almost barren.

I ate a lot of buttered pasta, but I also ate crab legs at an all-you-can-eat buffet with Haraboji (my paternal grandfather) and Korean hand-torn noodle soup, or *sujebi*, that Halmoni (my paternal grandmother) would make, while I sat cross-legged on the kitchen floor. I was picky, but I was also constantly surrounded by food, and all kinds of it.

Around the age of seven, though, I became afraid of food. I started to dread the Sunday breakfast table, and I would obsess over ways to make it look like I was finishing my dinner without having to actually eat it. I made lists in my Sanrio notebooks of excuses I could use to skip meals in dire situations and mastered the art of counting calories in my head. I was shrinking myself and slowly disappearing from family functions. I stuck to my safe foods, like unseasoned grilled chicken breasts, hard-boiled eggs, cucumber sticks, and oatmeal cooked with water only and four mini chocolate chips on top, no maple syrup or brown sugar.

After a decade-long battle with anorexia nervosa, coupled with a dependency on substances and alcohol, I adopted a vegan and mostly gluten-free lifestyle and finally learned to nourish myself in every sense of the word. I found my way back to the lacquered dinner table, and back to my roots.

Cats are imprint eaters, meaning they typically enjoy the same kind of food they ate as young kittens, and I've come to believe that we, as humans, are not all that different. At the height of my eating disorder, the food I dreamed about eating would always be things my mum had made for me as a kid, snacks my grandparents had prepared for me after school, and dishes I remembered eating during my family's moves and travels overseas. To this day, I most enjoy cooking the food that feels like home, the food my mum made for me growing up—and that inspires so many of the vegan recipes I create.

The recipes in this book each carry with them parts of my story. They have each been made possible thanks to the countries and cities I've lived in, by moments with my family members, and by the cultures they've passed down to me. And so, it felt fitting to share my own story of healing and reconnecting with my roots and the chapters of my life that led me to the vegan lifestyle through food.

what is vegan food?

I'm eight years into my vegan journey, and to this day my family members still get

confused sometimes and ask me whether or not I can eat peanuts or gluten, so here's a quick refresher for us all! A plant-based diet is one that excludes all animal products and byproducts (e.g., meat, fish, seafood, dairy, eggs, honey), but *veganism* is actually much more than just a diet or cuisine. It is a way of living that excludes animal products and byproducts from the plate as well as all other areas in life (e.g., not wearing leather or wool, not using beauty products formulated with animal byproducts, such as beeswax). I use the terms *plant-based* and *vegan* to describe the recipes in this book interchangeably, but all the recipes are completely vegan.

In Asian cuisines, heavy use of dairy products like milk, butter, and cheese is uncommon, but stocks and sauces tend to achieve their deep umami flavor with seafood, fish, beef, or chicken. In this book we'll replicate these flavors with some of nature's gifts, including, but not limited to, kelp, dried mushrooms, and miso paste.

Finally, while eating vegan does come with a set of parameters, you're never limited to one type of cuisine. With a little creativity in the kitchen, vegans can actually enjoy any cuisine. Don't give up your favorite dishes from your culture, and others—take inspiration from them instead.

how to use this book

My family likes to cook from the heart, without recipes. I encourage you to take inspiration from this and adjust everything *to taste*. When it comes to spice, salt, and sweetness in particular, everyone has a different preference, so don't be afraid to add or subtract as you see fit. It's useful to start with a light hand, though, because it's always easier to add more than it is to take away.

With that said, note that results will vary if you're making substitutions to foundational ingredients like flour (especially gluten-free flour) or swapping out a liquid sweetener for a granulated one. Some of the recipes in this book call for vegan and/or Asian staple ingredients you may not already have at home, and I strongly encourage you to check out your local Asian grocery stores, other international stores, health food stores, and Amazon or other online retailers to find the ingredients listed instead of trying an untested substitute. The difference between sriracha and gochujang is tremendous, for example, and will greatly change the outcome of the dish. I have included a few ingredient substitution notes where applicable, but I promise you'll use most of the staple ingredients more than once while cooking your way through this book, so it's worth the investment.

Nowadays, Asian ingredients are starting to become easier to find in conventional grocery stores, so chances are you can find most ingredients at your local shop!

If you're having trouble finding vegan ingredients, check health food stores and specialty grocery stores, like Sprouts and Whole Foods Market. Alternatively, there's a great selection from online retailers, too!

staple ingredients

While learning to cook vegan, I was introduced to a host of new ingredients that I had never used or even heard of before. After I removed gluten from my cooking as well, my ingredient vocabulary expanded even more! Here are a few key ingredients, including some Asian American staples, that are used throughout the cookbook, along with examples of how they are used and suggestions for possible substitutions.

AGAR AGAR This is a plant-based substitute for gelatin that is used as a thickening agent. It's derived from seaweed and used in a lot of Japanese desserts. I recommend using agar agar powder instead of flakes or sheets because it's easier to dissolve the powder into liquid quickly and evenly.

AQUAFABA Aquafaba is another name for chickpea brine, the liquid that comes in a can of cooked chickpeas. It is useful as an egg-white replacement: I use it in baking to make vegan meringue, and I brush it over baked goods before popping in the oven for that egg wash shine. You can make aquafaba at home by cooking your own chickpeas, but I've found the canned liquid to be much thicker and viscous.

BUCKWHEAT Although its name might suggest otherwise, buckwheat is a delicious gluten-free seed. You can enjoy it in the form of hulled kernels, called groats; whole seeds (as you would rice); or in flour form. I love consuming buckwheat groats toasted and crunchy as well as boiled and fluffed.

COCONUT SUGAR In many recipes, I use coconut sugar as a sweetener because it's unrefined and has a bit of a caramel undertone. Coconut sugar is commonly used in Southeast Asian cooking and desserts, and I honestly prefer its flavor over that of regular sugar. It can be used as a 1:1 replacement in most cases. Some recipes here do call for organic cane sugar, for example when you're brûléeing or making caramel, but in other cases you can feel free to use the sugar you prefer. Be aware when substituting that conventional sugar isn't always vegan due to the use of bone char to refine the sugar. If you want a similar taste and result, organic cane sugar is always vegan, as bone char is not involved in the process.

DAIRY-FREE DARK CHOCOLATE If a recipe calls for chocolate or chocolate chips, you can use any dairy-free chocolate. Most dark chocolates are naturally dairy-free, even if the label reads "may contain milk." That just means that the product was produced in a factory where milk products are also produced. In other words, don't worry about there being milk in the product; it's just a legal disclaimer.

DOENJANG PASTE This is the Korean equivalent of miso but with more funk and depth of flavor. It's not a popular ingredient outside of Korean cuisine just yet, but I absolutely love it, especially in brothy dishes like porridge. You can find doenjang paste at any Korean grocery store and most Asian grocery stores, too!

FIVE-SPICE Five-spice powder is a blend of various spices, including star anise and Szechuan peppercorns. It's used a lot in Taiwanese cooking and is often sprinkled on top of a finished dish.

FURIKAKE Furikake is a seasoning mix that often contains fish-based seasoning, seaweed, sugar, salt, and sesame seeds. In Japan, it's sprinkled on anything and everything! It's a staple condiment with lots of flavor. You can find vegan-friendly versions of furikake at most Asian grocery stores—just take a quick peek at the ingredient list!

GLUTEN-FREE FLOURS (BUCKWHEAT, OAT, CHICKPEA) In most of the recipes that call for gluten-free flour, I like to use Bob's Red Mill Gluten Free 1 to 1 Baking Flour because it contains a mix of various flours. The tricky thing about gluten-free baking is that you'll usually need to blend multiple flours to achieve a bouncy texture sans gluten, so using a 1:1 mix is a great way to cut down on time and ensure consistently good results. If gluten is not a concern for you, you can use all-purpose flour in place of 1:1 gluten-free flour in most of the recipes.

If a recipe specifies a specific type of flour (e.g., chickpea flour, tapioca flour), please don't substitute, as the specific variety is important to the recipe.

GOCHUJANG This staple Korean ingredient is a fermented red pepper paste that adds spice to a dish, but also some sweetness, savoriness, and umami. It's a very versatile ingredient and I'd highly recommend grabbing a tub to play with! Gochujang is at Trader Joe's stores now, but I have heard the flavor is on the mild side, so if you're able to find some at a Korean or Asian grocery store, I'd recommend buying it there instead. Gluten-free gochujang pastes do exist—just look for one thickened with rice flour in lieu of wheat.

LIQUID SMOKE This is a wonderful ingredient that really makes vegan meat substitutes more convincing. It adds a hickory smokiness that is hard to replicate otherwise. Just note that a little goes a long way.

MAPLE SYRUP I love using maple syrup as a liquid sweetener. It's a lovely, refined sugar–free option that works especially well for sweetening liquids. Be sure to find a pure maple syrup with no additional ingredients. You can also use agave in place of maple syrup in any recipe in this book.

MATCHA POWDER It's important to know that not all matcha is the same. While there are no certified guidelines to distinguish culinary- from ceremonial-grade matcha, ceremonial-grade matcha is considered higher quality. It's usually more vibrant in color, bolder in flavor, and much less bitter. It's typically made from the first harvest of the year, which means it's more nutritionally dense. I recommend always using ceremonial-grade matcha, as it will ensure a bolder color and flavor payoff when used in recipes.

MEDJOOL DATES This variety of dates is my go-to because they tend to be moister and larger than other varieties, with a caramel-like flavor. I prefer to purchase them unpitted, as having pits helps keep the dates moist. If you ever find that your dates are too firm, soak them in hot water for a few minutes, until soft to touch.

MIRIN This is seasoned rice wine vinegar with a little bit of sweetness. It's a great ingredient used primarily in Japanese cooking to build broths, sauces, and more.

MISO PASTE Miso is a fermented soybean paste that packs a lot of flavor. I love using it to add saltiness to dishes with more complex flavor profiles. There are a few varieties of miso paste you can purchase, notably white and red. Most of the recipes in this book that use miso call for white miso paste, which is a little milder than red and has a sweet note to it. You can find miso at most grocery stores these days. Experiment with miso instead of salt in other recipes and see how it works for you!

MUSHROOM POWDER Mushrooms are a staple in vegan cooking because they have a lot of deep umami flavor. You can think of mushroom powder as the vegan alternative to chicken bouillon powder—the idea is to use it to enhance the depth of flavor in savory dishes. You can find it at most Asian groceries or specialty grocery stores.

MUSHROOM SAUCE Mushroom sauce is a vegan alternative to oyster sauce, a staple in Chinese cooking. You can find a gluten-free variety these days, and it's amazing for seasoning stir-fries.

NEUTRAL OIL Neutral oil refers to an oil with a mild flavor and that typically has a fairly high smoke point. In other words, it won't alter the flavor of your dish and you can cook with it at high heats without worrying too much about smoking it. My favorite high-heat neutral oils are avocado oil and Zero Acre Farms cultured oil, a sustainable oil made from cultures and fermentation, but you can also use sunflower seed oil or vegetable oil. I do use olive oil in specific recipes, as it contributes more flavor to the dish, and I use toasted sesame oil as a finishing oil as it's super flavorful, but it burns quite easily so I don't cook with it.

NUTRITIONAL YEAST Nutritional yeast is a vegan's best friend, especially when making dairy-free cheesy things. It adds a nutty, yeasty flavor. When paired with the right mix of ingredients, you can use nutritional yeast to make vegan cheese sauces, cream cheese, and more.

PLANT MILK Feel free to use your favorite variety of plant milk in these recipes. Some will call for an unsweetened plant milk, meaning no added sugar and no extra flavoring. Some of the varieties I use the most are oat milk, soymilk, coconut milk, and almond milk.

RICE My family is passionate about rice. My dad, especially, is adamant about using a rice cooker for best results. Many of the recipes call for a side of cooked, short-grain white rice. You can absolutely substitute your rice of choice in most recipes, with the exception of the Crispy Rice Salad (page 73), which will be best with short-grain white rice that is a day old.

RICE WINE Rice wine, a.k.a. sake, is a cooking wine used often in Japanese recipes. You can substitute a different cooking wine, if preferred.

RICE WINE VINEGAR This is one of my favorite vinegars! It's lovely and mild and can be found at most conventional grocery stores. I use Mizkan, but any brand will do.

S&B CURRY POWDER S&B produces Japanese curry powder that is used to season the brand's pre-made Japanese curry roux packs. I love to purchase it as a powder because it's gluten-free (the pre-made packs are not). It's delicious sprinkled on popcorn, and I use it to season both squash soup (page 164) and a homemade Japanese curry (page 155). You're welcome to use a different curry powder if you're not able to find S&B, but do be aware that the flavor and end result of the dish may be quite different.

SESAME PASTE Chinese sesame paste is slightly different from tahini. It is usually thicker and richer in flavor while tahini is runnier and lighter. I do recommend looking for it at a local Asian or Chinese grocery store if you can! If not, tahini will do a fine job as a stand-in.

TAMARI This is my favorite gluten-free soy sauce alternative. It can be used 1:1 to replace soy sauce (which contains a small amount of wheat), but if gluten is not an issue for you, you can absolutely use regular soy sauce. If you're avoiding soy, you may want to consider using liquid aminos or coconut aminos.

TAPIOCA FLOUR Derived from cassava, tapioca flour, also called tapioca starch, is used in this book to make tapioca pearls for bubble tea (page 120) and in the Brazilian cheese bread (page 105). It has a gummy texture and cannot be replaced by other flours. It's also great for thickening.

TOASTED SESAME OIL This is a key ingredient in Korean cooking. Do make sure you use toasted sesame oil versus sesame oil, as it has more flavor. It is very strong, so always start with less and add more. As mentioned above, it burns easily so I use it mostly as a finishing oil.

TOFU There are many varieties of tofu, and each has its best use. I usually call for silken tofu, extra-firm silken tofu, extra-firm tofu, or high-protein tofu, listed here from softest to firmest. The texture differs based on the density of the tofu and how much water is in it. It's always a good idea to drain off the excess liquid the tofu is stored in and, if using an extra-firm or high-protein tofu, to pat it dry with a kitchen linen before using. Please pay close attention to the variety of tofu noted in each recipe, as the results will vary greatly based on what kind you use! For example, you must use extra-firm or high-protein tofu to make Popcorn Tofu (page 180); anything softer will fall apart.

TOGARASHI Togarashi is Japanese chili flakes. I love this ingredient and use it liberally when enjoying ramen or udon, but you can also use it to season veggies and more. You'll be able to find *ichimi* togarashi (single-ingredient chili powder) and *shichimi* togarashi (which contains seven ingredients, including citrus peel). Togarashi differs from Korean and other chili powders, so if you can find it, great! If not, gochugaru, red chili flakes, or Aleppo pepper flakes will also work.

VANILLA BEAN PASTE You can use pure vanilla extract as a 1:1 replacement in any recipe that calls for vanilla bean paste, but if you're able to find vanilla bean paste, I highly recommend it. It has much more flavor and includes real vanilla bean pieces.

VEGAN BUTTER A few recipes call for vegan butter, which helps add richness without dairy. You'll want to make sure you use a vegan butter that is firm at room temperature, not one labeled "spread." Spreadable vegan butters tend to melt at room temperature, meaning your recipe will be difficult to execute and may not turn out right. I really love using good old Earth Balance sticks and Violife's plant-based butter when cooking.

tools and equipment

BAKING PANS I recommend using metal baking pans where possible because they conduct heat well. Glass and ceramic bakeware can drastically change the results, especially with baked goods. Stick to metal where you can!

DEHYDRATOR This is a completely optional piece of equipment that is used in only one recipe: the Beetroot Flax Crackers on page 94. You can replicate the effect of a dehydrator in a standard oven by baking at the lowest temperature possible for a few hours.

FOOD PROCESSOR When working with a small volume, a food processor does an excellent job of breaking things down. I especially love making small-batch sauces in a processor.

HIGH-POWERED BLENDER I use a Vitamix blender because it's really powerful. For ingredients that are harder to break down, you might consider using a tamper to help. Otherwise, take breaks while you're blending to scrape down the sides of the container.

INSTANT POT/RICE COOKER As mentioned earlier, my dad feels strongly about rice cooking methods and swears that using a rice cooker is the best way to cook short-grain white rice (in his opinion, the only rice that matters). I will say it's a great hands-off method and the results are close to perfect every time. But I've heard you can also make amazing rice in an Instant Pot or pressure cooker! Of course, you can always use a plain old pot on the stove.

KITCHEN BLOWTORCH This is a common tool at many sushi restaurants and in

Japanese cooking. My grandma breaks out hers often. A blowtorch instantly adds a nice char to any dish you're cooking. I find mine handy and think it's a great investment for any home cook, but you can also broil things in the oven to replicate the same effect, or, if feasible, cook them over the open flame on a gas stove.

MANDOLINE Using a mandoline is the best way to get even, super-fine slices. It can be dangerous, as the blade is extremely sharp, so I recommend wearing a safety glove or using a safety guard when handling. It's not a necessity, but it will really make your life easier, especially when you're prepping a large quantity of thin slices (e.g., thinly sliced potatoes for Spicy Scalloped Potatoes, page 190).

MICROPLANE A Microplane or other fine grater helps you zest fruit, grate nuts and whole spices, and more.

NONSTICK BAKING MAT I love my nonstick mat because it's a reusable (and very nonstick) alternative to parchment paper, but parchment paper works just fine!

NUT MILK BAG OR CHEESECLOTH These are handy for straining homemade nut milks and removing the finest of pulp from blended mixtures. A nut milk bag is easier to work with because the ends are tied, but if you can't find one, your grocery store should carry cheesecloth, which works just as well. Just be sure to use a generous amount and hold its edges together tightly when squeezing so that no pulp escapes.

1 | **first things first**

One of my first food memories takes place in a modest apartment in Edgewater, New Jersey, where my family lived. I'm no more than four or five years old and eating one of my repeat breakfasts—a toasted Eggo waffle with a small scoop of Breyer's vanilla ice cream on top. I wait until the ice cream is melty, but not all the way melted, and use my Sesame Street knife to evenly distribute the ice cream so that each perfect square in the waffle has exactly the right amount of ice cream in it. I look forward to the weekend IHOP trip with my dad's side of the family, where I'll order the same exact thing I order every week: silver dollar pancakes with extra butter, because I'm not a maple syrup girl like Mum is.

When I was growing up, Asian breakfast food was not nearly as fascinating to me as American breakfast food. It's not that I loved American breakfast food all that much. In fact, there were a lot of things I *didn't* like. Bacon never appealed to me; the yolks of eggs were my worst enemy; I pulled the ham out of my McDonald's Egg McMuffin. I tried my best to like the fun breakfast foods that came individually wrapped in boxes, but I usually never made it past eating half of one serving before I decided I wanted nothing to do with it.

Still, I was fascinated by the shiny foil wrappers of Pop-Tarts, wanted to play every game on the back of the General Mills cereal boxes, and *really* wanted to like the powdered strawberry milk I begged my parents to buy. My friends loved all things

boxed and I felt I should, too, but aside from waffles and pancakes, I was really quite picky. The icing on the Pop-Tarts was too sweet, I didn't like that the Cocoa Puffs turned my milk into chocolate milk, and I preferred a glass of plain whole milk, without the clumpy powder bits at the bottom of the glass. Pancakes and waffles were some of the few "American" foods that I really enjoyed. Apple Jacks cereal also made the cut because I had fond memories of eating it with my dad. But really, I ate a lot of Asian breakfasts—especially when I spent time with my grandparents, and even more so after my first sister, Chloe, was born.

In most Asian countries, there isn't much discrimination between breakfast food and food eaten at other meals. Common breakfast items include hot foods like soup and porridge, and rice is also often served. My *obā-chan* (maternal grandmother) would make me miso soup, with perfectly circular shimeji mushrooms from a can that were slimy in the best way, always with a side of rice served in a lacquered red bowl. When we weren't at IHOP with my *halmoni* (paternal grandmother), she would make me egg-battered tofu served with a side of *kong bap*—purple rice with barley and beans.

After Chloe was born, my fascination with American breakfast food started to fade. I was in the first grade and both my parents were working full-time jobs. My mum left the house as early as five in the morning most days to start her commute, so we were lucky to have Sung Halmoni live with us part-time. She was a brazen Korean woman with the classic Asian grandma–style permed hair. She asked us, or rather told us, to call her Halmoni and made us kimbap for breakfast. Every single morning, I ate the freshly cooked rice wrapped in toasted seaweed that she'd rubbed sesame oil onto with her calloused hands, then performed the ritual of checking my teeth in the mirror for any seaweed remnants before the school bus came to pick me up.

One day after school, I came home and gobbled up my leftover breakfast kimbap as an after-school snack. My mum was home and asked what I thought about our family living in Taiwan. I ran upstairs to look at a map of the United States, scanning it furiously for this unknown place. *Taiwan.* I had never heard of it before and decided that it might be near Florida, one of the few places outside of New York and New Jersey that I had been to. I know what you're thinking— how does a part-Taiwanese person *not* know what or where Taiwan is? The answer to that is (1) I was maybe seven years old, and (2) the United States was really all I had ever known. Despite our mixed Asian heritage, I was born and raised in America; English was my first language and all we spoke at home.

I left for Taiwan with my mum and Chloe, and after a total of twenty hours sitting in an airplane, interrupted by an overnight layover in Seattle, it became clear to me that we were not going to Florida at all. We met my dad at Taoyuan International Airport (which at the time was still called Chiang Kai-Shek Airport) in Taipei, and the signs written in Mandarin looked more like art or graffiti than words to me. Among the crowd, I thought I heard a recognizable word or two—things my grandpa would shout into the phone— but eventually the sounds of the language started to fade into a dull background buzz. We left the baggage claim and a bouquet of new smells hit me. The hot and humid Taiwan air had a savory scent with notes of cinnamon, nutmeg, and warm spices that I had never smelled in combination before.

As we walked with our rolling suitcases closer and closer toward the smell, I could make out a small convenience store and what looked like a vat of steaming soup. I watched as patrons helped themselves, putting sausage-shaped skewered foods and pink-and-white speckled balls that looked like doughnut holes into to-go containers. We hopped into the car that would take us to our new "home." My eyes were glued to the window the entire ride, trying to make sense of this strange new place. As we neared the apartment, the streets began to narrow. Almost every single street was lined with carts selling food I couldn't identify. I thought to myself, *Right on the street?* It wasn't anything like a New York City hot dog or chicken-over-rice street cart situation. These were restaurants without walls, plastic stools of all colors strewn about and spilling into the road, red-and-white striped awnings housing each vendor. Baskets of eggs, vegetables, and noodles sat directly on the street in bright red and green plastic baskets. Produce was washed in colanders, with the water running right off into the gutters. Then, at the end of the road, I smelled it for the first time. Chloe and I covered our noses and mouths with both hands, taken aback by the pungent aroma. *Chou dou fu.* Stinky tofu.

We spent our first few days exploring the street vendors in our neighborhood. It was impossible not to walk by at least a few, no matter where you were headed. My favorite time to walk through was in the morning, when lines formed around the *dan bing* (egg pancakes) stalls in particular. I loved watching the scallion pancakes fry and curl up and the speed with which the Taiwanese *ayis* (aunties) would crack eggs right on top with just one hand. Bags of soymilk were tied at the top, looking like cotton candy at a New Jersey county fair. Perhaps the most fascinating to me were the *you tiao*, the big sticks of fried dough, each about a foot long, served alongside porridge and often dipped into the soymilk. It didn't take long for us to start digging into the local cuisine. I soon found that I absolutely loved *guo tie*, the 20NT (about $0.60USD) crispy potstickers sold down the block from our apartment, and we all took a strong liking to *tsua bing*, a shaved ice dessert with toppings varying from sweet beans to grass jelly. The most exciting discovery, however, was a little expat store called Tasters. It was right around the corner from my school and had rows of American candy sitting beneath the register. On the second floor, we recognized even more familiar labels like Jif peanut butter and Kraft macaroni and cheese, all labeled with outrageous prices. The first time we visited, we left the store with an overpriced box of Bisquick, and pancakes-from-the-box became one of our most comforting breakfasts, because they tasted like home.

just-add-mylk pancake mix

I love the convenience of just-add-milk pancake mixes from the box, so I was inspired to create a homemade version. You can prep the dry mix in advance (and double-, even triple-batch it), and when you're ready to enjoy, simply add your plant milk of choice and get to flipping! I love topping the pancakes with vegan butter, maple syrup, and seasonal fruit.

MAKES 8 PANCAKES, FOR 4 SERVINGS

DRY MIX

2½ cups oat flour

½ cup superfine blanched almond flour

¼ cup cornstarch or arrowroot starch

2 tablespoons coconut sugar

1 teaspoon baking powder

½ teaspoon baking soda

½ teaspoon kosher salt

PANCAKES

2 cups unsweetened plant milk of your choice

1 tablespoon neutral oil (see page xvi)

Vegan butter or more neutral oil, for greasing

1. To prepare the dry mix, sift the ingredients into a medium bowl and whisk to combine. You can store the mix in an airtight container in the refrigerator for about a month.

2. To make the pancakes, in a medium bowl, pour the plant milk into the dry mix and whisk until smooth. Let the batter sit to hydrate for 5 to 8 minutes, until thickened slightly.

3. Heat a large nonstick pan over medium heat and grease with vegan butter or neutral oil. Pour ¼ cup of the prepared batter into the center of the pan. When bubbles start to form on the surface and the edges start to brown, flip the pancake and cook for another 1 to 2 minutes, until lightly browned on the bottom. Repeat with the remaining batter.

WAFFLES

MAKES 8 WAFFLES, FOR 4 SERVINGS

To make waffles, prep the batter as above but add an additional 6 tablespoons neutral oil with the plant milk. Grease your waffle maker and add ¼ to ⅓ cup batter to the iron (adjusting the size depending on the size of the waffle maker). Waffles typically take 4 to 6 minutes to cook, but I recommend checking at around the 4- to 5-minute mark. The steam should start to disappear, indicating that the moisture is being cooked off and resulting in a crispier waffle! Repeat with the remaining batter.

park family pancake bake

This breakfast–dessert hybrid is one of the easiest ways to make pancakes for the family because it's one large pancake baked on a sheet pan. Everyone can customize a corner of the pancake with their toppings of choice, or you can bake it plain and offer a toppings bar. When we made a version of this when I was a kid, I would always opt for something chocolatey, my sisters loved berries, my mum loved sliced banana, and my dad always enjoyed the reserved plain quadrant of the pancake. Other topping options include seasonal fruit, nuts, sprinkles, dried fruit, and seeds.

MAKES ONE 13 X 18-INCH PANCAKE, FOR 4 TO 5 SERVINGS

Cooking spray (see page xvi) or vegan butter, for greasing

Just-Add-Mylk Pancake Mix (page 6), prepared through step 2

1 cup blueberries, optional

¾ cup dairy-free chocolate chips (I like the Enjoy Life brand), optional

1. Preheat the oven to 350°F.

2. Grease a 13 x 18-inch sheet pan with cooking spray. Gently pour the batter in and tap the pan on a hard surface to release any air bubbles.

3. Sprinkle the toppings of choice evenly over the batter. Bake for 10 to 12 minutes, until the pancake is cooked through and a toothpick inserted in the center comes out clean.

4. To serve, slice into squares and add any other desired toppings.

tomato toast

All it takes is one perfectly ripe, peak-of-the-season tomato to change your worldview. Raw tomato was never my favorite, until I fell in love with the beautiful heirloom tomatoes from the farmers markets in Los Angeles. I could eat them plain on toast with nothing more than olive oil, salt, and pepper—but we're going to level it up a little more. This is a no-cook, 5-minutes-or-less breakfast or snack I reach for whenever I can get my hands on a gorgeous tomato. Any tomato (or variety of them) will do, so use what you have or what's in season!

MAKES 1 SERVING

1 slice bread of your choice

Neutral oil (see page xvi), if pan-toasting

1 to 2 tablespoons Miso Butter (page 13)

½ medium heirloom tomato (a beefsteak tomato will also work wonderfully), sliced thick

Pinch of flaky salt, or to taste

Freshly ground black pepper, to taste

Red chili flakes, to taste

1 teaspoon grated fresh lemon zest, plus more to taste

Extra virgin olive oil, for drizzling, optional

Toast the bread in a toaster, or in a pan with a touch of neutral oil, until golden brown. Spread a generous layer of miso butter on one side. Place two or three slices of the tomato on top of the toast. Season with salt, pepper, chili flakes, and lemon zest and finish with just a drizzle of a high-quality olive oil, if desired. Eat immediately!

miso butter

I love to throw miso into any recipe I can. It's an underrated ingredient that most people consume exclusively by way of miso soup. But it has a really complex flavor profile: salty, slightly sweet, and deeply umami. The combination of miso and butter can take a simple recipe to the next level, and you can use the butter in place of conventional butter in any application. Spread it on toast, drizzle it on popcorn, bake with it, sauté with it, and more.

MAKES ¾ CUP, FOR TWELVE 1-TABLESPOON SERVINGS

8 tablespoons (1 stick) unsalted vegan butter, at room temperature

¼ cup white miso paste

1. In a stand mixer fitted with the whisk attachment or with a whisk in a medium bowl, whip the butter and miso paste together until smooth and nicely incorporated.

2. Transfer the mixture to an airtight container to store. Alternatively, you can spread it in a thick line on parchment paper, roll into a log shape, and tightly twist the ends. Or, melt and divide among the wells of an ice cube tray to create individual pats. In any case, let the butter chill in the fridge for 3 hours or overnight, until firm, before using. Store in the fridge for 3 to 4 weeks or in the freezer for 2 to 3 months.

miso-glazed mushroom toast

For my savory breakfast lovers, this umami bomb is for you. Mushrooms are a vegan's best friend; smear Miso Butter (page 13) on your toasts for even richer flavor.

MAKES 1 SERVING

Neutral oil (see page xvi)

1 slice bread of your choice

1 teaspoon white miso paste

1 teaspoon tamari

1 garlic clove, minced

½ cup thinly sliced fresh shiitake mushrooms

½ cup fresh oyster mushrooms

½ teaspoon kosher salt

3 tablespoons Vegan Ricotta Cheese (page 179), plus more to taste

Sesame seeds, for garnish

Scallions, thinly sliced, for garnish

Watermelon radish, cut into matchsticks, for garnish

1. Heat 1 tablespoon oil (or you can use vegan butter here) in a small pan over medium heat. Toast the bread in the pan until both sides are crispy and slightly golden brown, 2 to 3 minutes. Remove the bread and set aside; reserve the pan.

2. In a small bowl, mix together the miso paste, tamari, garlic, and 1 teaspoon oil.

3. In the same pan over medium heat, add enough oil to coat the pan. Add the mushrooms, season with the salt, and cook for 2 to 3 minutes, until the mushrooms are tender, glossy, and have shrunk slightly. Reduce the heat to low and add the miso sauce to the pan. Toss and cook the mushrooms and sauce down for another 2 to 3 minutes. The mushrooms should be glossy, soft, and fragrant.

4. To assemble, spread a generous amount of vegan ricotta on the toast, pile the mushrooms and sauce on top, and garnish with sesame seeds, scallions, and watermelon radish.

not-your-average avocado toast

There are a few things I really dislike paying for at restaurants and cafés, and one of them is avocado toast. The size of the serving is always unpredictable, the toppings and seasonings are often disappointing, and the price ranges anywhere from $10 to $20 (and then some, if you happen to want it on gluten-free toast). This at-home version has much more flavor to offer than the lemon juice, chili flakes, salt, black pepper, and olive oil that are usually added to toast. You'll get umami, spice, crunch, heat, and brightness in each bite, and you can adjust everything to your taste!

MAKES 2 SERVINGS

1 teaspoon tamari

½ teaspoon toasted sesame oil

½ teaspoon Everything Bagel Chili Crisp (page 192)

Juice of ½ lime

1 large ripe avocado, halved, pitted, peeled, and finely diced

2 slices bread of your choice

½ sheet nori, shredded or cut into thin strips (or use kizami nori), for garnish

1 teaspoon toasted sesame seeds, for garnish

1 scallion, thinly sliced, for garnish

Kosher salt, to taste

Freshly ground black pepper, to taste

1. In a medium bowl, whisk together the tamari, sesame oil, chili crisp, and lime juice. Add the avocado and gently toss to coat.

2. Toast the bread in a pan or toaster until golden brown.

3. Spoon a heap of the seasoned avocado onto each slice of toast, then garnish with the nori, sesame seeds, and scallion. Season with a generous amount of salt and pepper.

vegan cream cheese

There are two ways to make a simple vegan cream cheese and both start with a base of cashews and extra-firm tofu, taking inspiration from the tofu cream cheese option offered at most New York and New Jersey bagel shops! The first method requires some patience and fermentation and the second method is simply to season with lactic acid, which adds that tanginess that dairy cream cheese has. My personal favorite is to combine both methods, as given here. A little fermentation, a little lactic acid, and you have a vegan cream cheese that rivals the store-bought options. You can find lactic acid at some specialty culinary stores and online. It's a magical ingredient that I'd recommend for any vegan "cheese" making. Mix in additional ingredients for flavor, as in the variations that follow.

MAKES 2 TO 3 CUPS

1 cup raw cashews

Filtered water

One 15-ounce package extra-firm tofu

1 teaspoon kosher salt, plus more to taste

1 teaspoon lactic acid, plus more to taste

1 capsule vegan probiotic

1. Place the cashews in a small bowl and add filtered water to cover. Refrigerate for at least 2 hours, preferably overnight. (Alternatively, you can boil the cashews in a small saucepan in water to cover for a few minutes to soften until fork tender, then let cool.) Drain off the excess water and place the cashews in a high-powered blender.

2. Pat dry (but don't press) the tofu and add to the blender along with ¼ cup filtered water, the salt, lactic acid, and the inner contents of the probiotic capsule. Blend until completely smooth, making sure no lumps remain. Taste and adjust the salt and lactic acid as needed.

3. Transfer the mixture to an airtight jar, leaving about a quarter of the jar empty to give the mixture room to expand. Seal and let sit in a warm environment out of direct sunlight for 12 to 24 hours, until there are bubbles throughout and it is as tangy as you like. The longer you ferment, the more sour the cream cheese will be. If a skin forms at the top, skim it off and discard, then stir the mixture. Store in the refrigerator in an airtight container for 1 to 2 weeks.

cinnamon bun cream cheese

2 tablespoons pure maple syrup, plus more to taste

1 teaspoon vanilla bean paste

½ teaspoon ground cinnamon

¼ cup finely chopped walnuts

Prepare Vegan Cream Cheese (page 18) as directed in the high-powered blender, then blend in the maple syrup, vanilla bean paste, and cinnamon. Stir in the chopped walnuts.

strawberry cream cheese

⅓ cup freeze-dried strawberries

2 tablespoons pure maple syrup, plus more to taste

1 teaspoon vanilla bean paste

1 teaspoon freshly squeezed lemon juice

Prepare Vegan Cream Cheese (page 18) as directed in the high-powered blender, then blend in the strawberries, maple syrup, vanilla bean paste, and lemon juice.

garlic-chive cream cheese

Cloves from 1 garlic head, peeled

2 teaspoons extra virgin olive oil

Pinch of kosher salt

10 to 15 fresh chives, minced

Prepare Vegan Cream Cheese (page 18) as directed in the high-powered blender, then blend in the garlic, olive oil, and salt. Stir in the chives.

strawberry
cream cheese,
page 19

cinnamon bun
cream cheese,
page 19

vegan
cream cheese,
page 18

garlic-chive
cream cheese,
page 19

dirty jersey diner plate

Before we made our move to Taiwan, I spent many afternoons at Halmoni's wedding dress shop, Joyce Wedding. Halmoni always spoke to me in a mix of Korean and English. Most of her clientele was Korean and many of the surrounding businesses in Palisades Park, New Jersey, were Korean, too. Halmoni and Haraboji often picked me up from the Montessori school in Fort Lee for the afternoon. I was small enough then to hide underneath the fluffy skirts of the wedding dresses on display. In the center of the store, there was a round bridal riser, the little step in front of the mirror that brides-to-be could stand on as they tried on dresses. We often threw a patchwork blanket over it in between dress fittings and sat around it, cross-legged, eating our after-school snacks.

Some days we'd eat kimbap from the snack shop around the corner and other days it was japchae. I'd always share my Go-Gurt with Haraboji even though he insisted on squirting it into a soup spoon instead of eating it straight from the tube. On certain special afternoons, I'd get to spend time with my older cousin, Audrey, and go for an adventure around the block. We'd eat buttered white toast in the back room of a shop next door—the owners were friends of Halmoni and Haraboji—or we'd buy Snapple iced teas at the bodega on the corner and sip them while we snacked on dduk (Korean rice cakes).

The last meal I can recall eating in New Jersey before we moved to Taiwan was at a diner. I don't remember what neighborhood it was in, but I do remember it having everything a good diner should have: booths with dark red and brown tufted leather upholstery, amber polycarbonate cups with ice cubes shaped like speed bumps, and the smell of burnt coffee in the air. I don't remember who we were eating with or what anyone else ordered, but I do remember splitting a plate of scrambled eggs, hash browns, buttered toast, and bacon with my mum (and by that I mean she let me eat all of the buttered toast). Diner food was never something I consciously craved until it was no longer something we could find.

Years later, when we were living in Taiwan, an American-style diner restaurant opened and my family and I were so enthusiastic and excited about it. But the food was very subpar.

My mum always told me to pay attention when food was mentioned in books and in movies, that scenes around meals were extraordinarily significant. Of course, at the time I rolled my eyes and never really took the time to try and understand what she meant, but now I understand that food is so much more than just food. It has the power to take us back to a specific moment in time, which is why sometimes a crappy and inauthentic take on diner food in a foreign country can be simultaneously disappointing and comforting. It evokes the nostalgia I'd feel whenever I enjoyed a bowl of *sujebi* (noodle soup) and can make my family be always willing to make the trek to Palisades Park just to eat it at a restaurant with metal chopsticks and strong barley tea.

When I drive through Palisades Park now, Joyce Wedding no longer exists, but almost all the retail signs are still written in Korean and the neighborhood has become one of the largest and fastest growing Korean enclaves in the US. It also remains one of the best places to find a good bowl of sujebi. This Dirty Jersey Diner Plate has all the diner classics but with even more flavor (and zero burnt coffee). I love the tofu scramble with smashed potatoes and shishito peppers, smoky tempeh bacon, and most important, buttered toast.

garlic smashed
potatoes with
shishito peppers,
page 28

smoky maple
tempeh bacon,
page 27

tofu scramble,
page 26

tofu scramble

Reminiscent of classic scrambled eggs, this is a great way to start the day. It's high in protein and one batch serves a few hungry humans!

MAKES 4 TO 5 SERVINGS

4 teaspoons nutritional yeast

2 teaspoons white miso paste

½ teaspoon garlic powder

½ teaspoon onion powder

¼ teaspoon smoked paprika

¼ teaspoon ground turmeric

1 teaspoon kosher salt, plus more to taste

Freshly ground black pepper, to taste

¼ cup warm water

One 15-ounce package extra-firm tofu

1 tablespoon neutral oil (see page xvi)

Black salt, to taste, optional for eggy flavor

Thinly sliced chives, for garnish, optional

1. In a small bowl, whisk the nutritional yeast, miso paste, garlic powder, onion powder, paprika, turmeric, kosher salt, and pepper with the warm water to create a paste.

2. Wrap the block of tofu in a kitchen towel or paper towels and gently press to remove excess moisture. Use your hands to crumble the tofu into pieces the size of Ping-Pong balls (they will break down further as they cook, so don't start too small).

3. Heat a medium pan over medium heat with the neutral oil and add the tofu. Let cook for 2 to 3 minutes, tossing occasionally, until heated through.

4. Add the seasoning paste, stir to evenly coat the tofu, and cook the tofu mixture for another 2 to 3 minutes, until the moisture in the pan is mostly absorbed. Adjust the seasonings to taste and finish with black salt and chives, if desired.

smoky maple tempeh bacon

I'll be honest, I was never really a fan of bacon before going vegan, so giving it up wasn't too difficult for me. With that said, I think what makes bacon so delicious is its bold flavor. It's deeply smoky, lightly sweet, and really umami. I've re-created that flavor profile, using meaty, protein-rich tempeh to make plant-based bacon strips that are perfect for salads, sandwiches, and all things breakfast.

MAKES 6 TO 8 SERVINGS

2 tablespoons neutral oil (see page xvi)

¼ cup tamari

1 tablespoon coconut sugar

2 teaspoons white miso paste

1 teaspoon liquid smoke

1 teaspoon smoked paprika

½ teaspoon kosher salt, plus more to taste

Freshly ground black pepper, to taste

8 ounces tempeh, sliced thin (the thinner you slice it, the crispier your bacon will be)

1. In a medium bowl, whisk together 1 tablespoon of the oil, the tamari, coconut sugar, miso paste, liquid smoke, paprika, salt, and pepper. Add the tempeh slices to the marinade, making sure each piece is coated, and let sit for about 10 minutes.

2. Heat the remaining 1 tablespoon oil in a large nonstick pan over medium-high heat until hot. Remove the tempeh strips from the marinade and place in the pan, making sure each piece is fully in contact with the bottom of the pan. Cook in two or three batches if needed. Cook for 3 to 4 minutes on each side, until golden brown. Add a few tablespoons of the remaining marinade to the pan with the bacon and cook until the marinade has reduced and the edges of the tempeh slices are slightly caramelized.

3. Transfer the bacon strips to a sheet pan or other heat-safe tray and char them a bit with a kitchen blowtorch. This step is optional but adds really nice flavor to finish.

garlic smashed potatoes with shishito peppers

Enjoy these crispy smashed potatoes for breakfast—or any other time of day. The shishito peppers add a nice hint of heat (but not too much).

MAKES 6 SERVINGS

Neutral oil (see page xvi), optional

Kosher salt

1½ pounds red potatoes

5 tablespoons olive oil

1 teaspoon garlic powder

5 ounces shishito peppers (15 to 20 peppers)

1. Preheat the oven to 425°F. Line a sheet pan with parchment paper or a nonstick baking mat, or grease it with neutral oil.

2. Bring a large pot of water to a boil with 1 tablespoon salt. Add the potatoes and cook until fork tender, about 20 minutes.

3. Drain the potatoes and gently pat dry with a towel. Transfer to the prepared sheet pan and use the bottom of a glass to smash them down to about ½ inch thick.

4. In a small bowl, mix together 3 tablespoons of the olive oil, 2 teaspoons salt, and the garlic powder. Drizzle the mixture over the smashed potatoes and use your hands to toss, making sure each piece is coated. Bake the potatoes for 13 to 18 minutes, until lightly golden brown and crisp around the edges.

5. Meanwhile, in a separate bowl, toss the shishito peppers with the remaining 2 tablespoons olive oil and a pinch of salt.

6. Toss the shishito peppers onto the sheet pan with the potatoes. Bake another 7 minutes, until the potatoes are crispy on both sides and the peppers are tender. Season with more salt as needed and enjoy.

buckwheat brekkie bowl

As a vegan for almost a decade, I've eaten more bowls of oatmeal than I can count. This buckwheat bowl is everything you love about oatmeal but with a new, toothier texture. You cook it as you would oatmeal and can customize it with your favorite flavors.

MAKES 3 SERVINGS

1 cup buckwheat groats

1 cup filtered water

1 cup plant milk of your choice, plus more for serving

2 teaspoons pure maple syrup, plus more for serving

1 teaspoon grated lemon zest, optional

½ teaspoon pure vanilla extract

¼ teaspoon ground cinnamon

Fruit and/or nuts of your choice, for serving

1. Heat a dry medium saucepan over medium-high heat and add the buckwheat groats. Toast for 1 to 2 minutes, until lightly golden and fragrant, shaking the pan frequently to avoid burning them.

2. Add the filtered water, plant milk, maple syrup, lemon zest, vanilla, and cinnamon. Bring to a boil, then reduce the heat to a simmer. Cover and simmer for 10 minutes. Remove from the heat and let sit for 8 minutes, covered, until the liquid has been absorbed and the buckwheat is tender.

3. Enjoy with additional plant milk and/or maple syrup and the fruit and/or nuts of your choice.

super scallion quiche cups

If Starbucks egg bites and scallion pancakes had babies, they would be these cups. Many vegan breakfast options are carbohydrate heavy, but this is an amazing way to sneak protein in, perfect if you're having an active morning. It's a great recipe to meal prep, store in the fridge for 3 to 5 days or the freezer for up to a month, and take to go.

MAKES 24 SMALL QUICHE CUPS

2 tablespoons neutral oil (see page xvi), plus more for greasing

1 leek, halved, cleaned well, and thinly sliced

½ teaspoon kosher salt, plus more to taste

1 bunch scallions (about 10), thinly sliced

One 15-ounce package extra-firm tofu

3 tablespoons nutritional yeast

2 tablespoons cornstarch

2 tablespoons olive oil

1 tablespoon unsweetened plant milk of your choice, plus more as needed

1 tablespoon white miso paste

½ teaspoon onion powder

½ teaspoon garlic powder

1. Preheat the oven to 350°F. Grease a 24-well mini muffin tin with neutral oil.

2. Heat the neutral oil in a medium skillet, add the leek and salt, and sauté until the leek is tender, 7 to 8 minutes. Transfer to a bowl and stir in the scallions.

3. In a food processor or high-powered blender, blend the tofu, nutritional yeast, cornstarch, olive oil, plant milk, miso paste, onion powder, and garlic powder. The mixture should be spoonable but not too runny. If the mixture is too thick, add another tablespoon of plant milk to help blend the mixture. Add more salt if needed.

4. Gently fold the leek and scallion mixture into the tofu mixture. Transfer the batter to the prepared muffin tin, filling each well completely.

5. Bake for 30 to 35 minutes, until the tops are golden brown and slightly firm. Let cool completely to set, then gently warm for a minute in the microwave or in the oven at 350°F for a few minutes before enjoying.

chocolate quinoa breakfast bowl

Even if you're not a big quinoa fan, I urge you to try this quinoa breakfast bowl! It's deeply chocolaty, and the earthiness of the quinoa enhances the flavor—it adds that je ne sais quoi that espresso does in a brownie recipe. Not only that, but it's a great alternative to oats, with beautiful texture and a little more protein to start the day.

MAKES 2 SERVINGS

½ cup uncooked quinoa

1½ cups filtered water

1½ cups plant milk of your choice

2 tablespoons pure maple syrup

2 tablespoons cacao powder

2 tablespoons unsweetened almond butter

1 teaspoon vanilla bean paste

¼ teaspoon kosher salt, or more to taste

Fruit and/or nuts of your choice, for serving

1. Rinse the quinoa under cool tap water and place in a medium saucepan with the filtered water. Bring to a boil over medium heat, then lower the heat to a simmer. Cook, stirring often, until the water has mostly cooked off, 10 to 12 minutes. Add ½ cup of the plant milk and continue to cook, stirring frequently, until all the liquid has been absorbed by the quinoa, 7 to 8 minutes.

2. Remove from the heat and add the remaining 1 cup plant milk along with the maple syrup, cacao powder, almond butter, vanilla bean paste, and salt. Stir to combine, adjusting the seasoning to taste. Top with the fruit and/or nuts of your choice.

korean porridge

Porridge is to my dad what chicken noodle soup is to many—the ultimate bowl of comfort for sick days and chilly weather. I love porridge because it's such a simple dish that is made in so many different ways (flavors vary not only by country but also by region) and it's relatively cheap to make. Not only that, it's *the* dish I make whenever I have leftover rice on hand. This Korean-style porridge features veggies, some toasted sesame oil for flavor, and a fermented soybean paste (doenjang), which is like a cousin to miso paste.

MAKES 6 TO 8 SERVINGS

2 teaspoons neutral oil (see page xvi)

½ small zucchini, finely diced

¼ white onion, finely diced

½ large carrot, peeled and finely diced

1 cup cooked short-grain white rice

3 cups vegetable broth

2 teaspoons tamari, plus more to taste

½ teaspoon coconut sugar

1 tablespoon doenjang (Korean fermented soybean paste), optional

Kosher salt, to taste

1 teaspoon toasted sesame oil

Ground white pepper, to taste

Roasted seasoned seaweed, for garnish

Thinly sliced scallions, for garnish

1. Heat the oil in a medium saucepan over medium heat. Add the zucchini, onion, and carrot and cook, stirring, for 2 to 3 minutes, until fragrant. Add the rice and cook, stirring, for another 2 minutes or so, just to toast.

2. Add the broth and bring the mixture to a boil, then lower the heat to a simmer. Cook the porridge down, stirring often, for 15 to 30 minutes, until the texture is to your liking and the rice has softened.

3. Stir in the tamari, coconut sugar, and doenjang, if using. Season with salt, toasted sesame oil, and white pepper and garnish with roasted seaweed and scallions.

chinese porridge

Here's another variation of porridge, with more of a Chinese flavor profile. It's all about the toppings—add chili crisp for spice, umami sprinkle for depth of flavor and crunch, and white pepper to warm it all up.

MAKES 6 TO 8 SERVINGS

2 teaspoons neutral oil (see page xvi)

One 1-inch piece fresh ginger, peeled and finely grated

1 scallion, finely sliced

2 garlic cloves, finely minced

1 cup cooked short-grain white rice

3 cups vegetable broth

1 teaspoon toasted sesame oil

1 teaspoon kosher salt, plus more to taste

Ground white pepper, to taste

Everything Bagel Chili Crisp (page 192), for garnish

Umami Sprinkle (page 76), for garnish

1. Heat the oil in a small saucepan over medium heat. Add the ginger, scallion, and garlic and cook, stirring, until fragrant, 2 to 3 minutes. Add the rice and cook, stirring, for another 2 minutes or so, just to toast the rice.

2. Add the broth and bring the mixture to a boil, then lower the heat to a simmer. Cook the porridge down, stirring often, until the texture is to your liking and the rice has softened, 15 to 30 minutes.

3. Season with salt and white pepper and garnish with chili crisp and umami sprinkle.

matcha and pistachio granola

This granola takes inspiration from a cereal my family enjoyed when we spent time in Thailand. My mum would always say it was a *different* way to get your greens in. The granola is crunchy, packed with pistachios, and dusted with vibrant matcha powder. The nutty flavor of the pistachios is balanced by the grassy notes in the matcha, and the whole thing is sweetened with a little bit of maple syrup! You can use it to top a smoothie or dairy-free yogurt, enjoy it with milk, or eat it by the spoon- or handful.

MAKES 6 TO 8 SERVINGS

¼ cup pure maple syrup

⅓ cup unsweetened creamy roasted almond butter

1 teaspoon pure vanilla extract

Pinch of kosher salt

2 cups rolled oats

⅓ cup buckwheat groats

2 teaspoons ceremonial-grade matcha powder, plus more for dusting

⅓ cup shelled pistachios, chopped

¼ cup shredded unsweetened coconut, optional

1. Preheat the oven to 325°F. Line a sheet pan with a nonstick baking mat or parchment paper and set aside.

2. In a large bowl, whisk the maple syrup, almond butter, vanilla, and salt until smooth. Add the oats and groats and toss until the dry ingredients are well coated. Sift the matcha powder over the mixture and stir with a spatula to incorporate.

3. Transfer the mixture to the prepared sheet pan and use the spatula to spread it evenly, making sure there are no large clumps (this will help the granola to cook evenly and crisp up nicely!).

4. Bake for 10 minutes. Add the pistachios, toss, and bake for another 10 to 12 minutes, until golden brown. Let cool completely. Dust the entire tray with a little bit of matcha powder to finish and add shredded coconut, if desired. Transfer to a jar or airtight container to store in a cool, dry place for up to a week. Be sure to keep away from sunlight, otherwise the matcha will oxidize and the green color will fade.

2 | **salads that don't suck**
(and other delicious vegetables)

Romaine lettuce, eight to ten English cucumber slices, one heaping scoop of suspiciously yellow corn, a light tong-full of cheddar cheese shreds, and a white paper bowl and black plastic fork. This was lunch on repeat for a few years, beginning in the third grade.

I was above average in height compared to my classmates, even in the third grade, and described by the local Taiwanese mums as "bigger" than my peers. To this day, I'm still not sure whether they were referring to my height or my weight, because comments about appearance, including weight, are culturally very normal in many Asian countries. It was not stated in a hushed tone but in a matter-of-fact way, right in front of me, and in conversation with me, even. This prompted me to start looking at my body in comparison to other bodies around me, and I was, in fact, "bigger" than the other girls. I especially noticed this at my gymnastics team practices. My skin folded in some areas where the leotard met my body, and being taller than the rest of the team certainly made it hard not to feel big.

I don't really know when my new eating habits started, but I remember my parents receiving a call from the school. They were worried about my lunch choices and noticed that my friends started to mirror my lunches and frequent the salad bar, too. I began to feel nervous every time I entered the cafeteria, as if eyes were tracking my daily food selection, and made sure to opt for the hot meal lunch menu instead. I'd find ways to push the rice around the turquoise melamine tray in an effort to make it look like I had eaten my lunch, without really having to take a bite. I remember the ritual of watching *America's Next Top Model* after school, jogging in place in front of the TV and switching to jumping jacks for the commercial breaks. Eventually I stumbled across website forums suggesting that cucumbers and celery were negative calorie foods that required more calories to chew than they supplied.

By sixth grade, I had transitioned to eating primarily cucumbers and learned to convert the kilograms on our home scale to pounds. I packed the cucumbers in my backpack as a "snack" (when they were really my lunch), to be accompanied by the several bottles of water I would chug to try to feel full. My wardrobe became a rotation of long pants and the three sweatshirts I owned, despite the sweltering climate in Taiwan. I didn't want to hide that I was losing weight, but rather how big I felt. As I continued to grow, it became harder to keep up with sports, focus in class, and make excuses for my bizarre eating habits. I tried calling myself vegan, not really understanding what it meant other than that lots of foods were off-limits. I used it as an excuse to refuse food at parties and hangouts, and I'd always tell my friends I had eaten before I got there, only to get home and tell my parents that I had eaten with my friends. I gravitated toward the foods I'd see labeled *low-fat* and *low-carb*, like cold-cut turkey sandwiches made with the shelf-stable bread that came wrapped in plastic and boasted *only* 45 calories a slice and the 100-calorie snack pack versions of Oreo cookies. I could only dream about eating noodles and rice, thanks to articles in magazines that told me most Chinese food was "greasy and carb-heavy" and should be put on the "what not to eat" list.

After our next move, to Shanghai when I was twelve, I became friends with a group of girls who were athletes with great relationships with food. As a result of my new friends and the inevitable onset of puberty, my food practices became less and less extreme. In Taiwan, I could make it to 3:55 p.m. on the dot without eating before my stomach started to growl too loudly to hide it and I'd feel sharp pains in my abdomen. But my methods became impossible to hide after we moved to Shanghai. I sat at a cafeteria table alongside friends who'd completely devour the food on their plates and, even if I could skip lunch, it was difficult to make it through the school day and then volleyball practice with so little food in my system. As I got older and more involved with sports, my habits became more moderate out of necessity, but my relationship with food was still deeply disordered, and calculating carbs and calories consumed my mind. By the time my high school graduation rolled around, I could finally admit to myself that I was struggling with anorexia nervosa.

My first year of college was incredibly stressful, but it was about so much more than my move back to New York or adjusting to campus life. I worried about what kinds of low-calorie foods I could find at the cafeteria and how I could fit my lengthy cardio workouts into my schedule between classes and my campus job. It was around the same time that I went through many different iterations of the vegan diet after watching a documentary about the negative environmental impact of animal agriculture. First, I was simply vegan, then raw vegan, followed by fruitarian (fruit only) and SOS-free (salt-, oil-, and sugar-free). With access to a few free on-campus therapy sessions per semester, I started working through my eating disorder with a therapist and nutritionist at the medical services center and received a prescriptive vegan meal plan to stick to. I really did stick to the plan and eventually let go of some of my fear-based food restrictions on top of being vegan. This was because I finally came to understand that veganism was not a diet, but a lifestyle. It was about living compassionately, and food choice was simply *one* part of that lifestyle.

Conveniently, college was the first time I really had to cook for myself. Apart from cafeteria meals, I used the dorm kitchenette to try making vegan hand pies, tofu scrambles, and oat flour pancakes; I spent my free time with my hands deep in pizza dough. Cooking for myself became a form of exposure therapy. I was slowly overcoming my fear of food and actually starting to take interest and pride in learning how to make all things vegan from scratch, including bountiful salads that didn't suck, with dressing, no cucumbers, more than the four ingredients I had deemed "safe," and even a side of bread.

By the time college graduation neared, I had started making peace with food but still felt like an outsider at family meals. If we ate out, my order usually required modifications that I'd dread listing off to servers. Eating in was my preference because I could come prepared with a meal I had packed for myself in advance, so as to not inconvenience my family members. Even then, my single-serving vegan grain bowls and stir-fried vegetables were an anomaly at the table, so I started preparing larger portions of my food to share with the family. The idea was to hide my strange vegan food among the other dishes we were sharing so that I, too, was eating what everyone else was—but the food wasn't immediately a hit. It was the first time my family had ever tried things like cheese made from cashews or tofu in place of meat, and the dishes I made, though vegan, were inherently very Western foods.

I wanted so badly for my family to approve of this food, this lifestyle that had truly healed me. I rummaged through Obā-chan's kitchen, looking for something familiar I could make vegan. The first dish that finally wowed the family was a vegan "cheese" made with a little bit of miso paste in it—and when I say wowed, I mean they went in for seconds. While they didn't exactly have any complimentary words, they didn't have any critical notes to share about the dish either. That in itself was the best feedback I could have asked for. My family has always had thoughts about food being too salty, too sweet, too spicy, or too crunchy, so when it was quiet at the table, I knew the food was truly something special.

green garden soba noodle salad

Combining noodles and fresh veggies, this salad is the best of both worlds. Toss with the Tamari Vinaigrette for a light and fresh salad or the Miso Tahini Dressing for a creamier bite.

MAKES 1 SERVING

5 ounces soba noodles (or as much as your heart desires), cooked according to package instructions

1 Persian cucumber, thinly sliced or diced

½ ripe avocado, diced

1 scallion, green part only, thinly sliced

½ cup cooked shelled edamame

1 or 2 breakfast radishes, thinly sliced

3 to 4 tablespoons Tamari Vinaigrette (page 79) or Miso Tahini Dressing (page 78), to taste

Juice of ¼ lime

1 teaspoon toasted sesame seeds

1 sheet nori, crushed, optional

1. Place the noodles in a large bowl. Top with the cucumber, avocado, scallion, edamame, and radishes.

2. Add the dressing of your choice, the lime juice, and sesame seeds and toss to combine. Garnish with nori, if desired!

broccoli stem and shaved asparagus salad

One culturally Asian value that I believe is especially found in older generations of Asian American immigrants is the desire not to waste, to save for later, especially as it relates to food. When both sets of my grandparents were newcomers to the United States, having enough food was an absolute concern, so each and every part of an ingredient was used (in sometimes very creative ways) before it became waste. Not only that, in many countries outside of the United States, grocery items are sold without quite as much processing and "cleaning up." It's rare to find packages of pre-chopped fruits and vegetables, skins and stalks removed. My mum grew up eating the green flesh of the watermelon (the part that's usually tossed with the skin) like cucumber, something she learned from her thrifty grandmother. In Asia, fish is almost always sold with the head on, and the eyeballs are actually a delicacy to be fought over. Even the bones and innards of animals are put to use. A whole chicken is much preferred to cleaned-up, nicely packaged chicken breasts in a Styrofoam tray. I remember my family treasuring whole animals for the extra parts, especially the "unwanted" ones, which made the most flavorful stocks and broths. I attribute my current attitude toward food and food waste to my family's mindset when I was growing up and, while I am no longer eating any animals or animal byproducts, I apply the same principles to the things I do buy. Though pre-cut and packaged mirepoix is tempting at times, it would feel like a cardinal sin to purchase it and miss out on the onion and carrot skins and celery "butts" that can be turned into broth.

This salad includes broccoli stems, an ingredient that's often cut off and thrown out without a second thought. While it's common to see broccoli crowns sold without the stem, if you find a head with the stem on, save it for this delicious no-waste dish!

MAKES 1 LARGE SALAD, FOR 2 TO 3 SERVINGS

2 broccoli stems

1 bunch asparagus

4 breakfast radishes, thinly sliced

Tamari Vinaigrette (page 79), to taste

2 scallions, green parts only, sliced diagonally, for garnish

1. Start by preparing the broccoli stems: Use a vegetable peeler to remove the tough exterior skin, then use the peeler or a mandoline to shave thin planks. Alternatively, you can thinly slice the peeled stem crosswise into small discs.

2. To prep the asparagus, use a peeler to remove any tough, fibrous parts at the base of each spear, then shave into long strips.

3. Prepare a large ice bath with a generous number of ice cubes. Toss in the broccoli, asparagus, and radishes. Let sit for 5 to 10 minutes, until the vegetables are nicely firm and crisped up, then drain and use a salad spinner to remove any excess moisture.

4. Place the vegetables in a large bowl, toss with the vinaigrette, and transfer to a plate to serve. Garnish with scallions.

salads that don't suck (and other delicious vegetables)

oi muchim,
page 55

sunomono,
page 54

pai huang gua,
page 57

cucumber salad, three ways

A variation of cucumber salad is a common side in every culture of mine. It's a refreshing and cooling salad served alongside all manner of main courses. I've consulted my family members, who never measure anything, for the following Korean, Japanese, and Taiwanese versions! They're all easy to make, with slight ingredient tweaks among them.

sunomono

Japanese *sunomono* (酢の物) is a salad of paper-thin cucumber slices seasoned with a combination of soy sauce, sugar, salt, and vinegar and garnished with toasted sesame seeds. It's the perfect complement to brighten rich and savory dishes.

MAKES 2 SERVINGS

1 tablespoon dried wakame or seaweed, optional

2 small Persian cucumbers or 1 medium Japanese cucumber, thinly sliced on a mandoline

½ teaspoon kosher salt

1½ tablespoons rice wine vinegar

1 tablespoon organic cane sugar

½ teaspoon tamari

2 teaspoons toasted sesame seeds, for garnish

1. If using wakame, hydrate it by placing in a bowl with warm water and letting it sit for 10 minutes. Drain and use your hands to squeeze out as much liquid as possible. Set aside.

2. Place the cucumbers in a medium bowl. Add the salt and use your hands to make sure each piece is evenly coated. Let sit for 5 minutes. Rinse and drain the cucumbers to remove the salt, then squeeze between your palms to remove as much excess liquid as possible.

3. In a medium bowl, whisk the vinegar, sugar, and tamari. Add the cucumbers and wakame (if using) and toss to coat. Refrigerate for about 30 minutes if you prefer to serve chilled. Garnish with the sesame seeds and enjoy.

oi muchim

Korean *oi muchim* (오이무침) is a spicier, crunchier cucumber salad and includes a few more ingredients than Japanese sunomono. The flavor is bold but still refreshing, and this variation is delicious for those who like spice.

2 small Persian cucumbers or 1 medium Japanese cucumber, cut on a diagonal into ½-inch slices

⅛ small white onion, thinly sliced lengthwise, optional (my halmoni never included onions but many Koreans do)

1 garlic clove, finely minced

1 scallion, trimmed and thinly sliced

1½ tablespoons rice wine vinegar

1 tablespoon tamari

2 teaspoons organic cane sugar

1 teaspoon toasted sesame oil

½ teaspoon gochugaru

1 teaspoon toasted sesame seeds, for garnish

1. In a medium bowl, combine the cucumbers, onion (if using), garlic, scallion, vinegar, tamari, sugar, sesame oil, and gochugaru. Use your hands or tongs to toss everything together. Let sit for 5 to 10 minutes (in the refrigerator if you want it chilled).

2. Garnish with sesame seeds and enjoy.

pai huang gua

The thickest and crunchiest of these cucumber salads is the Taiwanese *pai huang gua* (派黄瓜). It calls for cucumbers that have been smashed or crushed, which results in a jagged texture that carries the sauce. It's typically garnished with cilantro and gets a spicy kick from chili crisp, chili oil, or chili flakes.

MAKES 2 SERVINGS

2 small Persian cucumbers or 1 medium Japanese cucumber

¼ teaspoon kosher salt

1 garlic clove, minced

1½ teaspoons tamari

1 teaspoon rice wine vinegar or Chinese black vinegar

¼ teaspoon toasted sesame oil

¼ teaspoon organic cane sugar

2 teaspoons Everything Bagel Chili Crisp (page 192) or 1 teaspoon red chili flakes

Handful of cilantro, torn, for garnish, optional

1 teaspoon toasted sesame seeds, for garnish

1. Start by cutting each cucumber lengthwise into three long pieces. Using a rolling pin or the blade of a knife, gently smash the pieces to flatten slightly and create jagged edges, then slice the long strips into pieces about 1 inch long.

2. In a medium bowl, combine the cucumber and salt and toss to coat. Let sit for about 10 minutes, then drain off any excess liquid.

3. In a small bowl, whisk the garlic, tamari, vinegar, sesame oil, sugar, and chili crisp or chili flakes. Pour the mixture over the cucumbers and toss. Refrigerate if you prefer it chilled.

4. Garnish with cilantro (if using) and toasted sesame seeds and enjoy.

quinoa salad

Here's a refreshing and low-effort salad that's perfect for the warmer months and makes for a great quick lunch. I'm not usually a fruit-in-salad person, but this salad pairs perfectly with the Raspberry Poppyseed Dressing, which adds just the right amount of tang.

MAKES 2 SMALL SERVINGS

1 cup halved cherry tomatoes

2½ cups baby arugula

1 small Persian cucumber, finely diced (about ¾ cup)

½ cup cooked quinoa

3 to 4 tablespoons Raspberry Poppyseed Dressing (page 80), or more to taste

In a large bowl, combine the tomatoes, arugula, cucumber, and quinoa. Mix using tongs or your hands. Add the dressing and toss again.

snap pea slaw

This delicious slaw is a more flavorful alternative to your average cabbage slaw and delightful to eat on its own. Plus, snap peas are one of my favorite vegetables, especially to eat raw. Of course, you can use most raw crunchy veggies in place of the snap peas (such as cabbage, cucumbers, or broccoli), but I've always loved the look of snap peas when sliced diagonally, and I adore the texture of the skin and the inner pea. This is a no-cook, five-minute recipe that I promise you'll make on repeat.

MAKES 3 TO 4 SERVINGS

1 pound sugar snap peas, trimmed and thinly sliced on the diagonal

½ large watermelon radish, julienned, optional

1 large garlic clove, finely grated

Juice of ½ lime

1 teaspoon rice wine vinegar

1 teaspoon kosher salt, plus more as needed

½ teaspoon toasted sesame oil, optional

In a large bowl, combine the snap peas, radish (if using), garlic, lime juice, vinegar, and salt. Toss to mix well, then season with more salt as desired. If you'd like, you can finish with a drizzle of toasted sesame oil.

five-spice brussels sprouts

Five-spice was a mysterious flavor to me before my family moved to Taiwan. There, it is liberally used, especially sprinkled on top of Taiwanese street snacks like popcorn chicken, grilled mushroom skewers, and other night market food. The spice blend is made up of star anise, fennel, cinnamon, Szechuan peppercorns, and cloves. Grind up the spices yourself for a more intense flavor, but you can also purchase the blend as a pre-made seasoning. I always describe it as the classic taste of Taiwanese street food in a bottle, and it's delicious on more than just fried chicken! If you're not a Brussels sprouts fan, feel free to switch them out for another hearty vegetable.

MAKES 2 TO 3 SERVINGS

2 tablespoons neutral oil (see page xvi)

1 pound Brussels sprouts, trimmed and halved

2 garlic cloves, minced

2 scallions, finely chopped

1 small dried bird's eye red chili or other dried red chili

2 tablespoons chopped roasted peanuts

½ teaspoon kosher salt

2 teaspoons tamari

½ teaspoon coconut sugar

½ teaspoon five-spice powder

¼ teaspoon ground white pepper

Fresh cilantro, for garnish, optional

1. Heat a large skillet over medium-high heat and add the oil. Swirl the pan to evenly coat the surface, then toss in the Brussel sprouts. Let sit undisturbed for about 4 minutes, then use a spatula to stir. Cook for 3 minutes, until the Brussel sprouts are lightly tender and golden brown on the exterior.

2. Add the garlic, scallions, dried chili, peanuts, and salt and toss. Cook for 2 to 3 minutes, until the garlic is fragrant and the Brussel sprouts are tender. Add the tamari, coconut sugar, five-spice, and white pepper and toss to coat by shaking the pan. Taste, adjust the seasonings, and serve with cilantro, if desired.

crunchy togarashi asparagus

Roasted asparagus is good, but roasted asparagus with a little crunch and spice really does it for me. These asparagus spears are coated in a cornflake-togarashi crumb and finished with a splash of lemon juice and a sprinkle of zest.

MAKES 2 TO 3 SERVINGS

2 cups cornflake cereal

2 teaspoons togarashi

1½ teaspoons garlic powder

2 teaspoons kosher salt, plus more to taste

1 bunch asparagus

2 tablespoons neutral oil (see page xvi)

Grated zest and juice of 1 lemon

1. Preheat the oven to 400°F.

2. In a food processor, blend the cornflakes, togarashi, garlic powder, and salt until a rough crumb is formed to create your "breading."

3. Cut off the base of each asparagus spear and use a peeler to remove any woody bit at the bottom. Toss the asparagus with the oil on a sheet pan to coat generously, then toss with the breading to coat evenly.

4. Roast the asparagus for 10 to 12 minutes, until fork tender and the breading is golden brown. Note that the cooking time will vary based on the girth of your asparagus.

5. Top with the lemon zest and juice and, if needed, season with additional salt.

go-to garlicky greens

No matter what we're eating or where in the world we are, my mum always finds a way to have a big plate of garlicky sautéed greens on the table. It's something I've become accustomed to and arguably one of the easiest ways to get your greens in. This recipe is my formula for a delicious plate of greens. Adjusting it to your taste is highly encouraged, as is rotating the veg you use! My go-to greens are baby bok choy and pea shoots, but you can also use spinach, kale, or any variety of Asian greens, to name a few. If using more than one vegetable, start with the firmer vegetables first to avoid overcooking the more delicate ones.

MAKES 2 SERVINGS

1 tablespoon neutral oil (see page xvi)

2 or 3 cups chopped greens of your choice (keep in mind, some vegetables will shrink in volume drastically once cooked)

¼ teaspoon kosher salt, plus more to taste

1 garlic clove, grated

1 small bird's eye chili pepper, thinly sliced, optional

1 tablespoon tamari

½ teaspoon toasted sesame oil

1. In a wok or large pan, heat the oil over medium heat. Add the greens and sauté until bright green and vibrant, 2 to 3 minutes. Season with the salt, add the garlic and the chili pepper, if using, and stir. Cover and cook for 2 minutes, until tender.

2. Uncover and season with the tamari, sesame oil, and more salt, if needed. Toss to coat and serve hot.

charred cabbage

My obā-chan always says that cabbage is one of the best vegetables because it's both affordable and healthy. When I was a child, I always associated cabbage with cabbage soup because of that scene in *Willy Wonka and the Chocolate Factory*. It never really appealed to me in soups, as it is used in many Asian recipes, but with the right cooking method, cabbage is truly a treat. My personal favorite preparation method is charring. It tastes best when done on the grill, but for those of you without access to a grill (myself included), you can easily achieve a beautiful char on the stovetop, too. After charring, cabbage becomes beautifully tender on the inside, almost buttery with blackened edges to complete the package. Season with salt and pepper and a generous amount of chili crisp as I do below, or serve with Miso Tahini Dressing (page 78) or Carrot Ginger Dressing (page 82). Prepare to love cabbage!

MAKES 2 SERVINGS

2 tablespoons neutral oil (see page xvi), plus more as needed

½ head green cabbage, cut into 1½-inch-thick wedges

Kosher salt, to taste

Ground white pepper, to taste

Everything Bagel Chili Crisp (page 192), for garnish

1. Heat the oil in a large skillet over medium-high heat.

2. Lay the cabbage slices flat in the pan and press them down with a spatula. Cook for 4 to 5 minutes, until a nice char has developed (don't be afraid to let it sit to develop some nice color), then flip and repeat on the other side. If the pan looks dry, add more oil when you flip the cabbage.

3. Season with salt and pepper and garnish with chili crisp.

very green beans

Green beans really only grace my family's table around Thanksgiving time, but *these* green beans are a bright and fun alternative that you can enjoy year-round (take it from me—I make this dish on repeat). These beans are an absolute joy, and the monochromatic green looks great on the plate, too!

MAKES 2 TO 3 SERVINGS

1 tablespoon neutral oil (see page xvi)

½ pound French green beans (haricots verts)

2 garlic cloves, minced

½ teaspoon kosher salt

⅔ cup Scallion Pesto (page 71), plus more to taste

Grated zest and juice of ½ lemon

Freshly ground black pepper, to taste

Umami Sprinkle (page 76), for garnish

1. Heat the oil in a large skillet over high heat. Add the beans and sauté for 4 to 5 minutes, until slightly charred. Add the garlic and salt, toss, and cook for another 2 to 3 minutes, until the garlic is fragrant and the beans are cooked through.

2. Spread a generous amount of pesto on a serving plate and top with the green beans. Finish with the lemon zest and juice and season with pepper. Garnish with umami sprinkle.

crispy rice salad

This is a salad even salad haters will love. The crispy rice adds crunch and a little more heart to the dish, and the gochujang dressing is the cherry on top. This salad is best served immediately to ensure maximum crunch in the rice pieces.

MAKES 2 SERVINGS

Neutral oil (see page xvi), as needed

1 cup cooked short-grain white rice (day-old rice works best!)

Splash of toasted sesame oil

½ teaspoon kosher salt

7 ounces butter lettuce (about 1 head)

1½ cups roughly chopped raw sugar snap peas

1 large or 2 or 3 golf ball–size watermelon radishes, sliced into half moons

1 Persian cucumber, sliced into thin rounds

Gochujang Dressing (page 81)

1 or 2 scallions, thinly sliced

1. Pour enough oil into a medium pan to cover the surface and heat over high until nice and hot. Add the rice, flatten it into a thin pancake, and cook until crispy, a few minutes per side. Brush on sesame oil for flavor and season with the salt. Transfer the pancake to a paper towel to absorb any excess oil. Once cool, crush the pancake into small pieces.

2. In a large bowl, combine the lettuce, snap peas, radishes, and cucumber. Add the dressing to taste and toss, then add the crispy rice and scallions and toss again. Serve immediately.

scallion pesto

"Get her off the ice or I'm going to call the cops!"

Haraboji and I were pretending to be ice skaters, sashaying and flailing our arms on top of a New Jersey lake that had completely frozen over. My grandfather smiled, ear to ear, ignoring the man, and we continued to glide across the ice, farther and farther away from the man calling out to us.

Haraboji was a really funny man. He was the first family member to openly curse around five-year-old me, but only because he didn't know the gravity of the words he was saying. We'd run laps around the red rubber track at the Edgewater Community Park and he'd yell "geese shat!" every time we ran past the green-ish goose droppings on the grass. I couldn't help but laugh every time he said it.

At the time, he and Halmoni were working a dry cleaning and tailoring shop on the first floor of an apartment building. Halmoni placed avocado pits sprouting tiny green leaves in white Styrofoam cups along the windowsill of the shop, and Haraboji had a mini Whirlpool fridge nestled underneath the hanging garments. In it, there would always be a combination of Korean snack foods like kimbap and Jolly Pong (puffed, sweetened barley cereal) and American snack foods like strawberry yogurt with mix-in sprinkles and Cheetos (the crunchy kind).

My parents and I lived in Demarest, a few towns over from the dry cleaning shop, in a house with a huge backyard. Part of the roof was dome shaped, and the wall between the kitchen and garden had a milk door. The front lawn was wild, with grass blades nearly knee high and many weeds to be pulled. Halmoni discovered *pa*, or scallions, hiding in the long grass. We started plucking pa from the front yard, making sure to pull the entire bulb out of the ground. That, she told us, could be saved and eaten.

Soon after that, Haraboji got to work setting up a garden in the backyard. He'd swing by unannounced at any hour of the day or night to rake, dig, or till. In all our years living in that house, I'm not sure that anything in the garden managed to grow to harvest, but nevertheless, Haraboji took care of the garden like it was his job. Eventually, we moved to Taiwan and said goodbye to our Demarest home. Before we left, I hid a few spare bricks I found, along with some cicada shells and Pokémon cards, in the milk door space, hoping the next tenant's children might find them and enjoy them as much as I did. Within the first week, the tenants called my parents to complain about Haraboji. It turns out, he never stopped tending to the garden even though we had moved to another country.

Halmoni and Haraboji didn't speak as much English as my other family members and that's perhaps part of the reason they didn't always express their love verbally. It was easier for Haraboji to communicate through the grocery store trips he'd take me on, tending to the garden, and insisting that I eat a third or fourth bowl of rice at every meal.

I think of Haraboji anytime I cook with scallions. You can consider this recipe an edible love letter from me to you. To make the scallion pesto, we start with all the flavors of a classic pesto and go from there. In addition to charred scallions, we're adding garlic and seasoning with white miso paste and a little salt.

MAKES ABOUT 3 CUPS

1½ cups sliced scallions (from about 15 scallions)

2 cups fresh basil leaves

3 garlic cloves, peeled

Juice of 1 lemon

½ cup extra virgin olive oil

⅓ cup roasted cashews

2 tablespoons nutritional yeast

1 tablespoon white miso paste

1 teaspoon kosher salt, plus more as needed

1. Char the scallions using a kitchen blowtorch until fairly blackened and fragrant. Alternatively, char in a dry skillet over high heat.

2. Place the scallions and the rest of the ingredients in a high-powered blender or food processor and process until mostly smooth (or your preferred texture). Taste and adjust salt as needed. Store in an airtight container in the refrigerator for up to 1 week.

umami sprinkle

Some people like to put hot sauce on everything. But me? My go-to seasoning is this umami sprinkle. It's the answer when you need a little extra flavor and crunch, with savory notes from garlic, shallots, and dried shiitake mushrooms. All you need is one pot to make not only the most irresistible topper but some delicious infused oil to use in place of conventional oil, too!

MAKES ¾ CUP

4 garlic cloves, thinly sliced

¼ cup neutral oil with a high smoke point (see page xvi), or more as needed

3 shallots, thinly sliced into rings

½ cup finely chopped dried shiitake mushrooms

Kosher salt, to taste

Shredded nori, optional

Toasted sesame seeds, optional

Red chili flakes, optional

1. In a small saucepan over medium heat, combine the garlic with enough oil to cover. Stir constantly until the garlic starts to sizzle, then cook for 4 to 5 minutes, continuing to stir constantly, until it starts to turn golden brown. As soon as it starts to brown, use a slotted spoon to transfer the garlic to a paper towel to drain. It will continue to cook, so don't wait too long!

2. Place the shallots in the oil and cook, stirring constantly, until they start to brown, about 15 minutes or so. Again, use a slotted spoon to transfer to a paper towel.

3. Repeat to cook the mushroom pieces, stirring constantly until they are very lightly brown, 3 to 5 minutes. Strain immediately through a sieve and transfer them to a paper towel, reserving the oil to cook with or fry in again.

4. Transfer the garlic, shallots, and mushrooms to a food processor and add ½ teaspoon salt. Pulse to break the mixture down into a chunky crumble. Taste and add more salt if desired. If using, add the shredded nori, toasted sesame seeds, and chili flakes.

5. Store in an airtight container in the refrigerator for up to a week. Store the strained oil in an airtight container for a few weeks.

miso tahini dressing

Miso and tahini is one of my favorite flavor pairings! The rich, nutty, and creamy tahini mixed with the deep umami miso flavor is irresistible and great not only in salads but also on top of any roasted vegetables (including potatoes—yum).

MAKES ABOUT 1½ CUPS, FOR 4 TO 5 SERVINGS

1 cup hemp seeds

½ cup tahini, shaken or stirred until smooth

½ cup filtered water, plus more as needed

¼ cup freshly squeezed lemon juice

1 tablespoon rice wine vinegar

2 garlic cloves, peeled

1 tablespoon white miso paste

½ teaspoon kosher salt

Freshly ground black pepper, to taste

Combine all the ingredients in a high-speed blender and blend until completely smooth, about 60 seconds. If needed, add more filtered water to help blend and adjust to the desired consistency. Store in an airtight container in the refrigerator for up to 1 week.

tamari vinaigrette

This is one of my all-time favorite vinaigrettes to toss with almost anything and everything. Great on salads, with noodles, and most raw veggies, too. I think of it as my Asian-ish alternative to balsamic vinaigrette: It's just as versatile but with flavors from my cultures.

MAKES 2 SERVINGS

2 tablespoons tamari

4 teaspoons toasted sesame oil

4 teaspoons rice wine vinegar

Juice of 1 lime, or more to taste

2 teaspoons pure maple syrup

1 garlic clove, grated, or ½ teaspoon garlic powder

Combine all the ingredients in a mason jar or sealable container and shake to combine. Alternatively, you can blend in a high-powered blender for 30 seconds.

raspberry poppyseed dressing

Choose your own adventure with this raspberry poppyseed dressing—keep it bright and pink or add a little gochujang for some heat (just note that this will give your dressing a warmer, red-orange color). All you need to do is blend! It's delicious on (almost) any salad, but especially tossed with Quinoa Salad (page 58).

MAKES 1 CUP, FOR 6 TO 8 SERVINGS

1 cup fresh raspberries

½ cup extra virgin olive oil

2 tablespoons champagne vinegar

1 teaspoon freshly squeezed lemon juice

1 teaspoon Dijon mustard

1 teaspoon pure maple syrup

1 teaspoon kosher salt

Freshly ground black pepper, to taste

2 teaspoons gochujang, optional

1 tablespoon poppy seeds

1. In a high-powered blender, combine the raspberries, olive oil, vinegar, lemon juice, Dijon, maple syrup, salt, pepper, and gochujang, if using, and blend until well combined and smooth.

2. Adjust the seasonings to taste and stir in the poppy seeds. Use immediately or store in an airtight container in the refrigerator for up to 5 days.

gochujang dressing

This buttery, spicy, zesty sauce is definitely not your average salad dressing. I recommend tossing your favorite greens and veg with it or drizzling it over grain bowls, like Mum's Macrobiotic Bowl (page 143). You can also use it instead of traditional bibimbap sauce, or as a marinade for vegetables and tofu.

MAKES ABOUT ½ CUP, FOR 2 SERVINGS

¼ cup filtered water

2 tablespoons unsweetened cashew butter

1 garlic clove, grated

1 teaspoon grated fresh ginger

1 tablespoon gochujang

2 teaspoons rice wine vinegar

½ teaspoon sesame oil

Pinch of kosher salt, to taste

In a small bowl, whisk all the ingredients together until smooth. Adjust the seasonings to your taste. Store in an airtight container in the refrigerator for up to a week.

carrot ginger dressing

Obā-chan and Jichang make a thirty-minute drive to Allendale, New Jersey, almost every single Saturday without fail to eat at Masa's Sushi and Grill. There are restaurants closer to them that also serve decent sushi, but I think that what's most special about that particular restaurant is Masa himself. My grandparents always praise his good work ethic and his ability to pick the best and freshest fish for sashimi, and prefer evenings when Masa himself is behind the sushi counter. He'll sometimes send desserts to our table, on the house, and whenever my little cousins Pacifico and Kento come with us, he sends them home with little toys or Japanese candy. Whenever he is out of town, everyone comments that the food just isn't as good—it is missing something. Over the years of Saturday dinners, Obā-chan and Jichang have become as much friends of Masa's as patrons of his restaurant.

In my college years, I'd take the 1 train up to 168th Street to transfer for the A train to 175th Street. I'd stop into a bodega to get cash, buy a white chocolate macadamia Clif Bar, and end up with two singles to pay for the jitney across the George Washington Bridge. On the New Jersey side of the bridge, Obā-chan would pick me up, Jichang in the passenger seat, and we'd make our way to Allendale. Usually, Obā-chan and Jichang had seats at the sushi bar reserved, but on evenings I'd join, we'd sit at the table nearest to the bar. Their order was always up to Masa, but my order remained the same each week: avocado salad with carrot ginger dressing (it came with imitation crab, which Obā-chan would eat for me), miso-glazed eggplant, a cucumber roll, and an avocado roll. Even after graduation and through the COVID pandemic, I continued to make Saturday trips to New Jersey whenever I could. We'd order takeout and Obā-chan would make the hour-long round trip so that we could enjoy Masa's sushi at home. It's a ritual that kept my family close through the most uncertain of times.

This dressing is a re-creation of Masa's dressing that we love so much. While it's not traditionally Japanese, carrot ginger dressing is a staple on salads at most Japanese restaurants in the United States.

Serve the dressing tossed with your favorite greens, or over chopped iceberg lettuce, shredded carrots, shredded cabbage, and cucumbers for an authentic sushi restaurant house salad.

MAKES ABOUT 2 CUPS DRESSING, FOR 8 TO 10 SERVINGS

sesame, soy, spice

82

1½ cups chopped peeled carrot

One 1-inch piece fresh ginger, peeled

2 tablespoons minced shallot

¼ cup mirin

¼ cup filtered water

1½ tablespoons tamari, plus more to taste

1 teaspoon toasted sesame oil

Combine all the ingredients in a high-speed blender and blend until smooth. Adjust the seasonings to your taste. Store in an airtight container in the refrigerator for up to a week.

3 snacks that smile back

As a kid, the most exciting things about my brown paper sack lunches had nothing to do with the actual meal. Instead, I'd look forward to the drawing of the day—a doodle by my mother in colorful Sharpie marker—and the snacks accompanying my lunch. Growing up in America meant growing up in one of the greatest snack countries in the world. Snacks were omnipresent. We'd pack snacks for school, snacks for the car, snacks for the beach, snacks for airplane rides, and even snacks for emergencies that would easily fit into purses and backpacks. I remember looking forward to playdates at different friends' houses based on the quality of the snacks. Rosa's house always had the Goldfish I liked, Shoko's house had the Japanese soy sauce rice crackers, and Evelyn's was more of a Cool Ranch Doritos and Fruit Gushers household.

My personal favorite snacks contained plenty of "natural" flavors and a healthy amount of food dye. I especially liked the snacks my parents ate because part of the fun of snacking was snacking together. I ate neon orange Cheetos with my mum and remember the thrill of picking out peculiar-shaped pieces in the bag; I shared cheddar cheese–filled Combos with my dad on the way home from the 7-Eleven; and I always looked forward to the variety of roasted nuts I'd shell and eat with my aunt Ohmi.

The day before my first day of third grade in Taiwan, I went to a grocery store with my parents to look for school snacks and ingredients for my packed lunch. The

pickings were slim. There were endless flavors of chewing gum, dried plums, hawthorn flakes, and vacuum-packed black quail eggs, but nothing that felt familiar enough. I settled on Hi-Chew candy and Wang Wang crackers and made a mental note to ask for more than one cracker pack because each one had only two crackers, each about the size of a pink eraser.

I don't remember what I ended up bringing for lunch on my first day, but I do remember that there was no brown paper bag (we couldn't find them in stores in Taipei). We were herded straight from PE class to the cafeteria, so I didn't have a chance to grab my lunch, and I quickly realized that everybody ate the school lunch and nobody brought their own. I stood in line for the hot meal and held my tray up for some iteration of steamed rice with pork. Though the meal was good, even great, all I really wanted was a simple turkey sandwich and a snack.

My first real playdate in Taiwan was at Rebecca's house. I was over the moon when her parents let us know that there were snacks ready for us on the table. I don't know what I was expecting, but it was definitely not sliced guava with salted plum powder on top. The sliced guava made a second appearance at the house of another friend, Christine, except this time it was served with a side of *suan mei*, preserved salted plums. Christine shared with me that dinners were relatively light. According to her parents, it was a good idea to eat like a king for breakfast, a common man for lunch, and a pauper for dinner. I was nervous to have dinner at her home, wondering if I'd feel full enough.

I was nine years old when I started looking forward to our summers back in America. *Shape* and *People* magazine became my bibles, and I was drawn to covers that promised to share Cameron Diaz's diet and the secrets to Lindsay Lohan's drastic weight loss. I wanted nothing more than to look like my fellow Taiwanese classmates and found satisfaction and results by simply eating less, which I did until the sixth grade.

As middle schoolers, we were granted access to the snack bar after school. It looked like an American fast food or burger joint with heat lamp–topped stainless steel shelves housing golden French fries, Tater Tots, and chicken nuggets. To the left of the fried goods were pastries and large chocolate chip cookies that became an important part of my daily routine. I'd skip breakfast and push my lunch around its tray at school, and the hunger pangs would hit hard after the last period. To quell the pangs, I'd eat half a chocolate chip cookie that was the size of my face. Despite my fear of most foods, I'd always find comfort in those cookies. They'd get me through another few hours of after-school activities before I headed home for my light dinner of mostly soup.

Many years later, I started working with a therapist and nutritionist to heal my relationship with food, and snacks took on a completely new meaning for me. In this chapter of my life, snacks were a prescription. My food Rx looked something like this: *breakfast, snack, lunch, snack, dinner, and— you guessed it—another snack.*

My relationship with snacks has evolved many times throughout my life, but now I thank them for providing me comfort, a sense of home, relief, and ultimately healing.

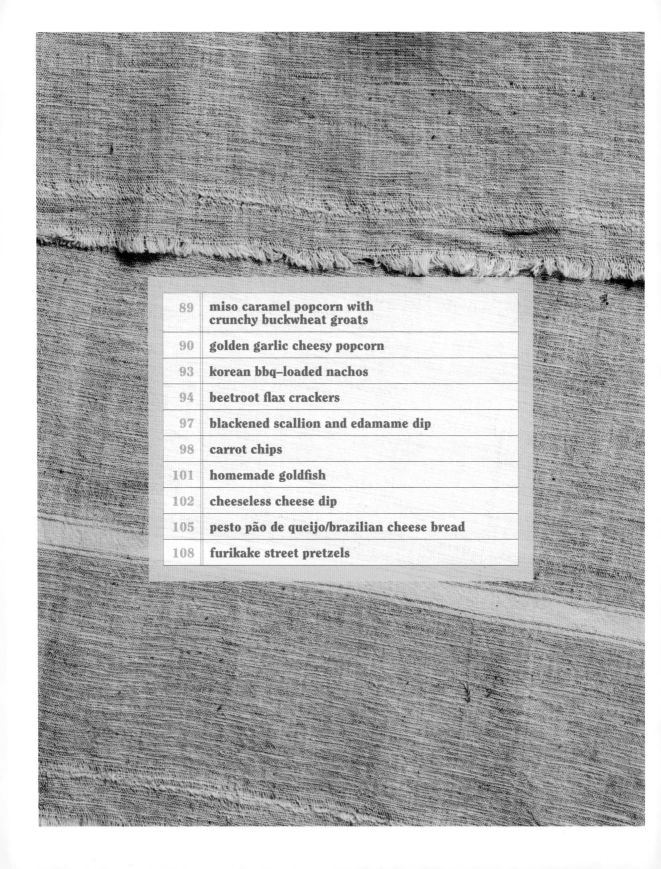

miso caramel popcorn with crunchy buckwheat groats

My French uncle Raba's guilty pleasure snack has always been an old-fashioned pack of Cracker Jack. He keeps his paper-clipped bag in the kitchen cabinet, right next to my aunt's roasted nuts. Every time I visit, he offers me a handful, without fail.

My homage to Cracker Jack, this toasty popcorn treat is coated with a crunchy layer of two-ingredient caramel, made with miso! The miso is used to mimic a salted caramel, but with even more depth of flavor, and the popcorn gets extra crunch from buckwheat groats. This is a hard caramel that has a nice crunch when cool and makes the perfect coating for popcorn.

MAKES 3 TO 4 SERVINGS

2 or 3 tablespoons buckwheat groats, optional

¼ cup filtered water

¼ cup organic cane sugar

2 teaspoons white miso paste

2 cups popped popcorn

1. Line a sheet pan with parchment paper or a nonstick baking mat.

2. If using, toast the buckwheat groats in a medium pan over medium heat, shaking constantly for 2 to 3 minutes, until fragrant and lightly golden in color.

3. Prepare the caramel sauce by combining the filtered water and sugar in a small saucepan over medium heat. Don't touch or stir the caramel; let it sit. You can gently swirl the pot if needed to help dissolve the sugar. Cook until it starts to darken in color, and then you can start to stir the mixture occasionally. As soon as the caramel becomes a deep amber color, remove from the heat and whisk in the miso paste until incorporated.

4. Place 1 cup of the popped popcorn and the buckwheat groats, if using, in a bowl, then quickly and evenly pour over the caramel. Toss with a spatula to distribute the caramel, then spread out the mixture on the prepared sheet pan. Let the caramel set and cool until crunchy.

5. Break up any clumps, then add the remaining 1 cup popped popcorn to the mix. Let the popcorn cool completely, then store in an airtight container for up to a week.

golden garlic cheesy popcorn

My mum has always loved popcorn. She gets a medium bucket of buttered popcorn at the movie theater, she packed white cheddar popcorn snack packs for my sisters and me, and she even took us to the candy store at the mall from time to time, where she'd fill a little cellophane bag with buttered popcorn Jelly Bellys. Buttered popcorn was a snack that I sincerely missed in my first few years as a vegan, but this version scratches the itch (and so much more) with rich, dairy-free miso butter, garlic, and nutritional yeast for that cheesy flavor.

MAKES 8 CUPS, FOR 3 TO 4 SERVINGS

1 tablespoon neutral oil (see page xvi)

¼ cup popcorn kernels

2 tablespoons Miso Butter (page 13)

2 tablespoons nutritional yeast

1 teaspoon garlic powder

Kosher salt, to taste

¼ teaspoon freshly ground black pepper

1. Heat the oil in a large pot over medium heat. Add the popcorn kernels, immediately cover with a lid, and cook the popcorn, shaking the pot every 30 seconds or so, until the popping slows. Remove from the heat and let sit for a few minutes, then transfer to a large bowl.

2. Melt the miso butter in a small saucepan over medium heat, then drizzle it over the popcorn, using a spatula to toss to coat. Add the nutritional yeast, garlic powder, salt, and pepper and toss to coat again. Enjoy immediately!

korean bbq–loaded nachos

I couldn't decide whether this dish belonged in the snack category or whether it should be counted as a meal, because I've certainly enjoyed eating these nachos for dinner many times. Either way, it's a delicious, share-friendly dish with crunch, creaminess, heat, chew, and bite. Get your hands in there!

MAKES 4 SERVINGS

6 ounces tortilla chips of your choice

Shredded Korean BBQ Bulgogi Tofu (page 152)

Cheeseless Cheese Dip (page 102), warmed

½ jalapeño chili, thinly sliced into rounds, optional

½ ripe avocado, diced, optional

¼ cup thinly sliced red onion or pickled red onion, optional

Cilantro leaves and/or sliced scallions, for garnish, optional

1. Spread the tortilla chips onto a sheet pan or serving tray.

2. Top with the bulgogi tofu, cheese dip, and any of the other toppings you like. Garnish with cilantro and/or scallions, if desired.

beetroot flax crackers

These beetroot crackers are (almost) too pretty to eat! You can prepare them two ways: Either dehydrate to maintain the stunning pink hue from the beets or bake in the oven for toastier flavor. Dip them into Blackened Scallion and Edamame Dip (page 97), Cheeseless Cheese Dip (page 102), or enjoy with your favorite soup.

MAKES 2 SERVINGS

1 cup blanched almond flour

2 tablespoons flax seeds

1 tablespoon black sesame seeds

One 15-ounce can cooked beets

1 teaspoon kosher salt

1. Preheat the oven to 350°F or a dehydrator to 115°F.

2. Toast the almond flour, flax seeds, and sesame seeds in a dry pan over low heat until fragrant and lightly golden, 3 to 5 minutes, shaking the pan constantly to avoid burning. Transfer to a medium bowl.

3. In a blender, blend the beets and the liquid from the can until smooth. Add ¼ cup of the beet mixture to the almond flour mixture and mix to form a dough. It should stick to itself and form a dense ball. You can save the remaining beet mixture for smoothies, soups, and more!

4. Place the dough on a long sheet of parchment paper and lay another sheet on top. Roll out the dough to about 1⁄16-inch thickness. Season generously with the salt. Cut the dough into any shapes you like (squares, triangles, or otherwise), or leave whole to bake, then break the sheet into crackers after baking.

5. Bake in the oven for 20 minutes or dry in the dehydrator for about 3 hours, until crisp.

blackened scallion and edamame dip

This green dip, high in protein and rich in flavor, comes together in 10 minutes or less. Taking inspiration from classic hummus, the dip is a puree of edamame beans and other Asian ingredients. Enjoy with Carrot Chips (page 98) or Beetroot Flax Crackers (page 94), or use as a spread for your favorite sandwich. It also stores well, so it can be made ahead for parties or even meal prep.

MAKES ABOUT 4 CUPS, FOR 4 TO 5 SERVINGS

8 whole scallions, plus thinly sliced greens for garnish

1 cup cooked shelled edamame beans

Juice of 1 lemon

2 garlic cloves, peeled

1 teaspoon toasted sesame oil, plus more for optional garnish

¼ cup Chinese sesame paste (see page xvii)

1 teaspoon kosher salt, plus more to taste

3 tablespoons extra virgin olive oil

½ cup ice water, plus more as needed

Toasted black and white sesame seeds, for garnish

1. Start by charring the scallions: You can use a kitchen blowtorch to char them on all sides, or a grill if you have one. Alternatively, char them in a dry heavy-bottomed pan over high heat until their exteriors are blackened, 5 to 6 minutes.

2. Place the scallions, edamame, lemon juice, garlic, sesame oil, sesame paste, and salt in a blender or food processor and blend until smooth. Continue to process while pouring in the olive oil, followed by the ice water, adding more as needed to achieve the desired texture (some like it smooth, some like it a little chunkier!).

3. Adjust the seasoning to taste. Garnish with sliced scallion greens and toasted sesame seeds, along with toasted sesame oil, if desired.

carrot chips

Legend has it that these chips may improve your eyesight. My entire family wears glasses or contacts of some kind, so unfortunately, we can't vouch for it, but they are delicious and worth making nonetheless.

MAKES 4 SERVINGS

1 pound carrots, peeled and sliced ⅛ inch thick on the diagonal

2 tablespoons neutral oil (see page xvi)

1 teaspoon kosher salt, plus more to taste

½ teaspoon garlic powder

¼ teaspoon smoked paprika

¼ teaspoon onion powder

¼ teaspoon freshly ground black pepper

1. Preheat the oven to 450°F.

2. Place the carrots in a medium bowl and toss with the oil and all the seasonings.

3. Spread the carrots on a sheet pan and bake for 12 minutes, until golden brown. Flip the carrots and bake for 12 minutes more, until golden brown and crisp on the edges. Let cool completely on a wire rack to crisp up further.

4. The carrot chips are best enjoyed immediately.

homemade goldfish

When you grow up on cheesy snack crackers of all kinds, it's hard not to want to find an alternative as an adult vegan. These little fish are a bit of a labor of love to prepare—with an eye and smile on each fish—but you can also cut the dough into simple squares if you want a snack in a flash (just don't expect them to smile back).

MAKES 4 TO 5 SERVINGS

1 cup chickpea flour

3 to 4 tablespoons nutritional yeast

1 teaspoon garlic powder

¾ teaspoon ground turmeric, optional

½ teaspoon baking powder

½ teaspoon onion powder

½ teaspoon paprika

1 teaspoon kosher salt

⅛ teaspoon freshly ground black pepper

1 tablespoon miso paste

¼ cup neutral oil (see page xvi)

¼ cup ice water

1. Preheat the oven to 325°F.

2. Place all the dry ingredients (through the pepper) in a food processor and pulse to combine. Add the miso paste and pulse to combine, then gradually start to stream in the oil while processing, followed by the ice water. Pulse until a dough starts to form and pull away from the walls of the processor.

3. Roll out the dough between two sheets of parchment paper to 1/16 inch thick and use a goldfish-shaped cutter to cut out fish. Poke an eye in each goldfish with the end of a skewer and make the mouth with a small spoon or other rounded edge. Because the goldfish are delicate, I recommend transferring the bottom sheet of parchment paper directly onto a sheet pan. Work any scraps back into a ball and repeat to roll and cut out the remaining dough.

4. Bake for 6 to 7 minutes, until golden brown and crisp. Be careful not to burn them, as they are quite thin! Cool completely and store in an airtight container in a cool, dry place for up to 2 weeks.

cheeseless cheese dip

I never would have believed that you could make a cheesy dip out of potatoes, carrots, and onions . . . but then I went vegan and started enjoying this cheeseless dip with anything I could think of. Turn it into a pasta sauce or thin it out with more water to drizzle it over broccoli for a nostalgic bite.

MAKES ABOUT 5 CUPS, FOR 4 TO 5 SERVINGS

1 cup diced peeled russet potato

2 cups diced peeled carrots

½ yellow onion, diced

5 garlic cloves, peeled

⅓ cup raw cashews

¼ cup nutritional yeast

1 tablespoon white miso paste

1 teaspoon garlic powder

½ teaspoon smoked paprika

1 teaspoon kosher salt

Juice of ½ lemon

1. Bring a small pot of water to a boil over high heat. Add the potato, carrots, onion, garlic, and cashews and cook until the potato and carrots are fork tender, 6 to 8 minutes. Reserve ½ cup of the cooking water, then drain off the rest. Transfer the cooked vegetables to a blender.

2. Add the remaining ingredients to the blender and blend until smooth. Add a bit of the cooking water as needed to adjust the thickness.

sesame, soy, spice

pesto pão de queijo/ brazilian cheese bread

When I was in college, my uncle Eugene opened his second restaurant, Cherry Izakaya, on North 8th Street and Bedford Avenue in Brooklyn (the restaurant has since been replaced by Egg Shop). At the time, Williamsburg was an up-and-coming neighborhood, with new restaurants opening all along the L train line. Eugene lived in an apartment with his then-girlfriend, Roberta, with rent almost as high as in Manhattan neighborhoods like the East Village and Chelsea. I loved spending my weekends in Williamsburg, commute and all, even though it was often difficult to balance my coursework, student job, and on-campus friendships. It was my escape from the college campus, and Eugene, along with my aunt Ohmi who lived in Manhattan, were the closest family I had since my parents and sisters were living in Shanghai. Some weekends, Obā-chan and Jichang would drive in from New Jersey, so I always made it a point to make my way to Williamsburg when they did. One evening, all five of us walked from Eugene's apartment to a Peruvian restaurant called Chimu. It must have been my first time eating Peruvian food because I unknowingly consumed both heart meat and blood sausage. I wasn't vegan yet, but I was also not the most adventurous eater, especially with organ meats. When I realized what I was eating, I shifted my attention to the yuca fries. In contrast, Roberta excitedly went not only for the heart and blood sausage but also the tripe. Obā-chan and Jichang smiled and nodded as Roberta ate.

Roberta is from Brazil, and while there are tremendous differences between Brazilian and Asian culture, there are a lot of similarities, too. One example, and perhaps something that helped win over my grandparents, is the food culture. In both Brazil and Asia, many parts of animals that are typically discarded in the United States are considered delicacies—things you'd offer a loved one. My family habitually offered shrimp heads to my mum and Eugene, and my grandparents always saved the fish cheek meat for my sisters and me. We were also offered the eyeballs . . . but none of us were ever too interested in them. Roberta, on the other hand, loved every centimeter a crab had to offer, enjoyed *karasumi* (Japanese bottarga) alongside Jichang, loved oxtail and jellyfish, and never let a fish eyeball go to waste. In other words, she could eat—and my family loved that about her. Nothing was too out there, and she'd try everything at least once.

Roberta also took an interest in my cooking. She would be the first to try my new vegan dishes, however unattractive or underseasoned they were in testing, and she'd help me read through Brazilian websites in search of ways to veganize classic Brazilian dishes like feijão tropeiro and pão de queijo. She'd go to the Brazilian grocery store to bring me sour manioc flour and all kinds of cassava products specific to Brazilian cuisine. Together we developed recipes to share on my blog, and we rolled and baked vegan pão de queijo in the kitchen of the New Jersey home she and Eugene had moved into. Sharing our cultural dishes, whether vegan or not, fostered a deep connection. Though I don't see Roberta often anymore, whenever I come across a Brazilian recipe on my Instagram explore page, my first thought is to forward it to her, and she remains my go-to for any questions about the cuisine.

Pão de queijo is a popular Brazilian bread with a bouncy, chewy texture, usually made with cheese. It's one of the first recipes we labored together to try to veganize and, surprisingly, is fairly simple to make. For extra fun flavor, I like to stuff the pão de queijo with Scallion Pesto (page 74) before baking, but you can omit the pesto for a more traditional bread that is just as delicious. The dough can also be prepared in advance and stored in the freezer. After you roll your balls of dough, spread them on a lined sheet pan, cover with plastic wrap, and freeze until solid. Once solid, transfer to an airtight container for storage until you're ready to bake.

MAKES ABOUT 25 PIECES, FOR 4 TO 5 SERVINGS

1 fist-size gold potato (you want to end up with 1 cup of mashed potato), peeled and quartered

⅓ cup olive oil

2 cups tapioca flour

¼ cup nutritional yeast

½ teaspoon garlic powder

¼ teaspoon onion powder

1 teaspoon kosher salt

1 cup Scallion Pesto (page 74)

1. Preheat the oven to 350°F and line a sheet pan with parchment paper or a nonstick baking mat.

2. Bring a large pot of water to a boil. Add the potato and boil until fork tender, 8 to 10 minutes. Reserve ½ cup of the cooking water and drain the potato. Transfer to a bowl and mash with a fork. Measure out 1 cup of the mashed potato and set aside. (If there is any extra potato, snack on it with a little bit of Miso Butter, page 13.)

3. Pour the reserved water into a large bowl and whisk in the olive oil.

4. In another large bowl, whisk together the tapioca flour, nutritional yeast, garlic powder, onion powder, and salt. Add the mashed potato mixture, work it in with your hands, then add the olive oil mixture. Start mixing with a spatula, then work the dough using your hands once it starts to form. It may feel a little dry at first; just be sure to keep packing the dough tightly until the olive oil is combined.

5. Form the dough into about twenty-five 1½-tablespoon balls. Flatten one gently and hold in your left (or non-dominant) hand. Place 1 teaspoon of pesto in the center and re-form the ball around the pesto, bringing the edges of the dough inward to create a tight seal. Repeat to fill all the dough balls.

6. Space half of the dough balls evenly on the prepared sheet pan, leaving at least 1 inch between each. Bake for 25 to 30 minutes, until the bottoms of the breads are golden brown and small cracks start to form on the surface. Repeat with the remaining dough balls. These are best enjoyed immediately.

furikake street pretzels

I was always fascinated by the street-cart pretzels you see all over Times Square. I wondered why and how the pretzels were all the same size, no matter which cart they came from, and whether one supplier was the pretzel plug for all the carts in Midtown. In the ninth grade, I finally decided to buy one; it felt like something I needed to do just once. It was bigger than my face and, as expected, dry and salty. These pretzels take inspiration from those ubiquitous New York pretzels, but they're better in my book: snack-size, fluffy, and seasoned with a generous amount of furikake.

MAKES 8 PRETZELS

1 teaspoon active dry yeast

⅔ cup warm unsweetened plant milk of your choice

2 tablespoons neutral oil (see page xvi), plus more for greasing

1 tablespoon pure maple syrup

2½ cups gluten-free flour (see page xv)

1 teaspoon kosher salt

¼ cup baking soda

Furikake, for topping

1. Start by activating the yeast: Combine the yeast, plant milk, oil, and maple syrup in a small bowl and let sit for 10 minutes, until frothy.

2. Combine the yeast mixture, flour, and salt in a stand mixer with a dough hook attachment and mix on medium speed until combined. Alternatively, you can mix the dough in a large bowl by hand, using a spatula.

3. Transfer the dough to a bowl greased with neutral oil and cover with a kitchen linen or other cloth. Let sit in a warm place to rest for 30 minutes to 1 hour. The dough may not rise very much, as gluten-free flour can be finicky, but the yeast also adds a depth of flavor to the pretzel.

4. Preheat the oven to 425°F and line a sheet pan with parchment paper or a nonstick baking mat.

5. Divide the dough into eight equal pieces. Roll out each ball into a log about 12 inches long. To twist into a pretzel shape, arrange the log in an upside-down U shape, then take the ends of the log and twist them together a few times. Pull the twisted ends upward and then press down lightly at opposite sides of the top of the curve to set in place.

6. Bring 8 cups water to a boil in a large pot and add the baking soda. One at a time, give each pretzel a 1-minute dip in the boiling water, then transfer to the prepared sheet pan. Sprinkle with a generous amount of furikake while still wet.

7. Bake for 12 to 15 minutes, until the pretzels are golden brown and cooked through. These pretzels are best enjoyed immediately, but you can store leftovers in an airtight container in the refrigerator for 2 to 3 days and reheat them in a toaster.

4 **crying over spilt soymilk**

I was thirteen years old the first time I set foot in a Shanghai nightclub. We'd been living in China for a little less than a year, and I quickly learned that going out to the bars and clubs was a normal thing for expatriate teens to do. I was nervous about whether I'd be turned away. I was tall for my age, but I still wore the highest pair of heels I could find, put on as much makeup as I reasonably could, and wore a snakeskin print halter top and white miniskirt to help me look old enough to be there. I packed lip gloss, a few hundred RMB, and a portable phone charger in a slinky gold crossbody bag.

I had butterflies, or maybe something more aggressive, like wasps, in my stomach as we made our way to the club by taxi. I didn't know the dance yet: Did they check your ID? I didn't have an ID. Did they ask you any questions at the door? Was the 200RMB open bar *really* unlimited? What do you do at the club? I approached the bouncer, handed him two of the pink bills with Mao Zedong's face on them, and felt a wave of relief wash over me as I made it past his gaze. The walls inside MAO, *or was it Muse?*, were made of black glittery tile, and the music was so loud that the beat pulsed right through me. The smell of cigarette smoke filled the air, and the floor was somehow both sticky and slippery. There were a lot of firsts that night.

It didn't take long for this to become routine. Each week from Wednesday through the weekend, I'd wonder which club and what party I'd be at. Faces in the crowd became friends I'd see only during the latter half of the week and exclusively after

11 p.m. Some nights it was Ladies' Night at the Bottle Opener Building (Shanghai World Financial Center), or free-flow frozen margarita night at Zapata's. I grew accustomed to going through the motions from Monday to Wednesday, dragging my feet at school, but the week always felt like it started Wednesday night. I loved the ritual of riffling through my closet, trying to figure out what to wear and looking for the highest heels I could manage walking in. I decided that my favorite drinks were the kamikaze shots at Windows Bar and the open-bar vodkas with lime. I would return home with my hair smelling like Marlboro Lights and whatever beverage had spilled on my shoes. Sometimes the breaks for air outside the club, cigarette in hand, were my favorite moments. It was quiet enough to have a conversation, and the midnight air felt good on sweaty skin.

If an early teen in eight-inch heels at a free-flow bar sounds like a recipe for disaster to you, I'd say you're not wrong. Nobody had an ID; instead, juniors and seniors at the school would become DJs or promoters with hookups at the club. Sometimes the bouncer would be the guy you sat next to in math class. Inside, you'd see not only your classmates but students from other international schools, too. The clubs were like a watering hole for all the expatriate kids from schools all over the city, and sometimes it was the only way you'd see your friends from the Shanghai American School campus in Puxi, or the Rego International School.

Over time, my favorite parts of the

night shifted from the getting ready and the dancing to the drinking and the drugs. It was easy to get your hands on drinks at free-flow bars with low prices. Older men would offer to buy drinks for you and your girlfriends, and you could even walk out of Lawson convenience stores with an 8RMB liter bottle of *baijiu*, no questions asked. Drugs were a little harder to come by, but there was always a friend of a friend who could find you whatever you needed if you knew the right people. By the time I entered high school, I had tried almost everything I could get my hands on, but the mystery white pills were easily my number one. It was what I was handed on my very first night out, which I would learn years later was ketamine.

I would wake up with bruises all over my legs, mascara down my face, presumably from crying, my iPhone glass screen often shattered. The morning after was like a game of Clue. I'd scroll through photos I had on my phone, read through my texts, and try to piece together the night. Slowly but surely, I was pushing the envelope.

I negotiated with myself along the way:

I'd never smoke cigarettes. They're so bad for you.

Honestly, smoking weed is healthier and more natural than cigarettes. At least it's not a pill!

Pills seem scary, but I'd never snort anything. That's really bad.

No matter what, I'll never inject anything.

At the same time, on paper, I was checking off all the Asian family boxes: I was still in school with an A average; I made the varsity dance team, mastered both French and Mandarin, always had my hair nicely styled for church no matter how hung over (and/or sometimes still high) I was from the previous Saturday night; and I was accepted at my target Ivy League school. I was the thinnest I had been, the drugs and alcohol aiding my efforts to eat less and shrink more, and photos of me from the clubs would make it on the Shanghai nightlife and entertainment websites. My club persona was fun; I was always on the dance floor with a drink in hand—outgoing, confident, and too high to be depressed or anxious. While my parents were certainly more Americanized than many Asian families, I had my act down for the sake of meeting the unspoken cultural expectations that come with being Asian. In my head, playing that part successfully felt like a pass for my behavior outside of school.

After my eighteenth birthday, I experienced a Very Bad Thing and started drinking alone. It was no longer just a social experience, but a way out. I'd long for the drowsiness I felt after drinking so I could sleep through the day. I wanted nothing more than to feel the MDMA euphoria without the comedown, so I just kept taking it to ride the high. By my senior year of high school, I had hit rock bottom. I was about to be a student at my dream school, but I was deeply dependent on both alcohol and a slew of substances. My math teacher, Mrs. Saich, let me excuse myself from Contemporary Math because I'd break into tears in the middle of class so often, and Mrs.

Hope let me hide out in the extracurricular support room, even though I wasn't one of the students on her roster. Somehow, I made it to graduation.

I like to joke now that unlike the rest of my peers in college, who were exploring drugs and alcohol for the first time, I was instead *un-learning* how to drink and use. In my first week in Manhattan, I opened up to my roommate about parties in Shanghai, thinking she'd be able to relate with stories of her own. Instead, I was met with wide eyes and a mouth agape.

My freshman year of healing felt like learning to surf. The path was never linear and the waves would often pull me under. Sometimes I'd work my way up to standing on the board, only to slip and fall again. Over and over, I'd walk by the church on 110th Street and pace back and forth on the sidewalk before deciding to walk back to my dorm room. But finally one day I went in—and attended my first AA meeting. Sitting toward the back of the room, I didn't participate, but I listened intently. There were mothers, bus drivers, teachers, and artists, and I was the youngest in the room by a long shot.

With every visit back to Asia during my summer and winter breaks, my circle of friends at school and back in Shanghai grew smaller and smaller. As a freshman, I was instantly drawn to people who partied and liked spending their evenings at Up & Down, Le Bain, 1 OAK, and the PHD Rooftop Lounge. In the summers and winters back in Asia, I'd fall back into my old routine, frequenting the same bars and clubs and throwing back cheap tequila. But by junior year of college, I had only a handful of friends that I felt comfortable spending time with. I'd go to my friend Rachelle's house and we'd do our nails together, watch old shows on bootleg streaming websites, make experimental vegan macarons, and chase her cats around the first floor. I'd try new restaurants, which was a huge part of the work I was doing to repair my relationship with food, and take aerial yoga classes (which were much more enjoyable and easy with proper fuel in my body) with Lisa. We'd have sleepovers in the living room and always ate pancakes slathered with Nutella the morning after.

Eventually, I started to look forward to midday runs to get bubble tea slushies and lattes with 3D foam art instead of nights fueled by screwdrivers and Bloody Marys. I became obsessed with drinks of all kinds— smoothies, sparkling waters, mocktails, cold-pressed juices, and tea. And as it turns out, there are actually a lot of fun nonalcoholic beverages you can enjoy when you're not living nocturnally.

street corner soymilk

Like many Asians, I have always had trouble digesting dairy. As a kid, I drank a lot of soymilk; it was always easy to find, especially when I was living in Asia. In the mornings, I'd walk by street stalls selling freshly made soymilk, usually served with *you tiao*, or fried dough sticks. Although soybeans get a bad rap in the United States, soymilk is one of my favorite plant-based milk alternatives because it's one of the highest in protein, is so creamy (no gums or fillers necessary), and is fairly neutral in flavor. That said, there's a huge difference between store-bought and fresh soymilk. You can buy fresh soymilk if you a tofu shop accessible to you. The flavor is incomparable. You can also try your hand at making fresh soymilk at home; it takes a little patience, but all you really need are soybeans and water.

MAKES 4 CUPS

1 cup dry soybeans

Coconut Sugar Simple Syrup (page 123), to taste, optional

1. Rinse the soybeans thoroughly and soak them overnight in room-temperature water.

2. The next morning, drain and rinse the soybeans, place them between two kitchen towels, and rub off as many of the skins as you can.

3. Divide the soybeans into four portions (so that there is ample room for blending). Place one portion in the blender with 2 cups water and blend until completely smooth. Transfer the liquid to a large pot. Repeat with the remaining portions.

4. Bring the soybean liquid to a boil, then lower the heat to a simmer. Let the milk reduce to the thickness of your liking, making sure to keep an eye on it as it can boil over quickly. I like to cook it down for 15 to 20 minutes, until rich and creamy.

5. To filter out the pulp, strain the milk through a cheesecloth or nut milk bag into a large pitcher or container. Be sure to squeeze the pulp to get all the liquid out. Add the coconut sugar syrup, if desired. The soymilk will keep in the refrigerator for about a week.

sesame, soy, spice

116

perfect pistachio milk

A smooth, creamy, naturally green nut milk! It pairs perfectly with lattes and cereal and is a delicious beverage to enjoy with cookies. For an even more vibrant green color, remove the pistachio nut skins by gently rubbing the soaked pistachios between two kitchen towels.

MAKES ABOUT 3 CUPS, FOR 3 TO 4 SERVINGS

1 cup shelled pistachios

3 cups filtered water

1 teaspoon vanilla bean paste

Pinch of kosher salt

Sweetener of your choice, optional

1. Toast the pistachios in a dry pan over medium heat for about 5 minutes, until lightly golden, shaking constantly to avoid burning. Transfer to a medium bowl of cool water and soak for at least 3 hours, or up to overnight.

2. Drain the pistachios. In a blender, combine the pistachios, filtered water, vanilla bean paste, and salt and blend until smooth.

3. Strain the milk through a cheesecloth or nut milk bag. Sweeten to taste, if desired, then store the milk in the fridge in an airtight container for up to a week.

homemade bubble tea

I was first introduced to bubble tea in Queens, New York, by my uncle Eugene. On my first sip I nearly choked on the unexpected pearl that lodged in my throat. Little did I know that soon after I would be moving to the bubble tea motherland—Taiwan. There, I walked past at least four bubble tea shops on my way to school every morning, each with a long list of drink variations including add-ins like *bu ding* (pudding) and chrysanthemum. Most afternoons, I walked home, up Yang Ming Mountain, to get bubble tea with friends. Bubble tea was present at every celebration we had at school, served as a snack the same way pizza or cans of soda might be at American celebrations. Bubble tea has to be the best representation of Taiwan in a drink. You can now find it served in creative ways all over the world, but the most classic iteration is simple: cold black tea, milk, and tapioca pearls.

MAKES 2 SERVINGS

TAPIOCA PEARLS

½ cup tapioca flour

1 tablespoon coconut sugar

TEA

2 bags black tea, or
2 tablespoons loose black tea of your choice

Ice

2 tablespoons Coconut Sugar Simple Syrup (page 123), or more to taste

2 cups sweetened or unsweetened plant milk of your choice

1. Start by preparing the tapioca pearls: Place the tapioca flour in a medium heatproof bowl and place the coconut sugar in a small pot. Bring a teakettle of water to a boil and pour 3 tablespoons of the boiling water into the sugar. Stir until completely dissolved. Bring the pot of sugar water a boil over low heat, then pour the hot sugar water into the bowl with the tapioca flour. Using a small spatula, stir until a sticky dough forms.

2. Transfer the dough to a work surface and divide into two parts. Roll out each into a long, thin strip about ½ inch thick. Cut into small pieces, about a ⅓ inch in length, and roll each piece into a tight ball. Depending upon your preference, you will want ¼ to ⅓ cup of cooked tapioca pearls per serving. Cook immediately or, to store for later use, let them sit on the countertop, making sure no pieces are touching, to air-dry overnight, until completely dry. Store in an airtight container in a cool, dry area or in the freezer.

3. Bring a medium saucepan of water to a boil over medium-high heat. Add the tapioca pearls and boil until they float and become translucent, about 5 minutes; they will cook quickly. Remove from the heat and let rest for 10 minutes, then transfer to a bowl of lukewarm water to keep them from sticking.

4. To prepare the black tea, bring 1½ cups water to a boil in a kettle or pot and pour it over the tea bags or leaves in a pitcher. Let steep for 5 to 10 minutes, to your desired strength. If using tea leaves, strain after steeping.

5. To assemble the drink, add ice to two tall glasses, followed by the cooked tapioca pearls. Spoon a tablespoon of simple syrup into each glass and top each with ¾ cup brewed black tea and 1 cup plant milk. Enjoy!

coconut sugar simple syrup

This staple sweetener can be used to enhance drinks of all kinds, including mocktails and matcha lattes. I love using coconut sugar (see page xiii) as the syrup base because it has a caramel-like flavor and is a great alternative to conventional sugar. If you'd like, you can even infuse the syrup with chamomile.

MAKES ABOUT 1½ CUPS, FOR 15 TO 20 SERVINGS

1 cup coconut sugar (use light golden coconut sugar for a syrup that's lighter in color and flavor)

1 cup filtered water

½ cup fresh or dried chamomile flowers, optional

Combine the coconut sugar and filtered water in a small saucepan over medium heat, bring to a low simmer, and simmer, stirring constantly, until the sugar is dissolved. Set aside to cool. (For chamomile syrup, add the flowers while the mixture is simmering. Cool, then strain out the flowers.) Store the syrup in an airtight container in the refrigerator for up to 3 weeks.

everyday matcha latte

When I was growing up, green tea and matcha were constantly around me. Tea culture in Asia is big in the same way coffee culture is big in other parts of the world. If you're enjoying a meal in Asia with tea service, it's incredible how the servers make sure that your cup is never empty. In fact—no matter how many sips you take—if you look away for one second, your cup will be brimming with hot tea. You'll find bottles of hot and cold teas at convenience stores in jasmine, black, red, and green varieties, and, of course, bubble tea shops are everywhere. My obā-chan loves green tea: Meals at her house are often followed with a hot cup of either genmaicha or sencha. She'll excuse herself to start clearing our plates, and on the way to the sink she switches on the electric kettle. She gathers mugs for everyone and starts steeping the special tea she brought from Japan that is saved in the freezer, all while continuing to chat with us from whatever part of the kitchen she is in.

In college I purchased Kirkland green tea bags so that I, too, could make myself cups of green tea after dinner at the dorm cafeteria, but the taste was disappointing. On the weekends, back at Obā-chan's, I compared green teas and sometimes left with some of her tea. Every Sunday, I asked her questions about the different varieties of tea, and at a certain point I exhausted her store of information. My thirst for knowledge and the tastiest tea continued to develop and I spent much of my time learning about tea, attending traditional Japanese tea ceremonies and even contributing to articles by news and media companies about matcha.

Now that I'm older, I scramble to clear the table at family meals and transport the dishes to the sink. On the way, I switch on the electric kettle pull out the matcha bowls, chasen (whisks), and mugs, and get to whisking a cup for everyone at the table. In recent years, both my grandma and aunt have developed a new love for matcha for health reasons, and I love bringing their tea to the table, just the way Obā-chan would.

MAKES 1 SERVING

½ to 1 teaspoon ceremonial-grade matcha powder, plus more to taste

⅓ cup hot (but not boiling) water

Ice, optional

1 cup plant milk of your choice

½ teaspoon pure vanilla extract or vanilla bean paste, optional

Pure maple syrup, optional

1. Start by sifting the matcha powder into a small bowl: Use a small scoop or spoon to push it through a sieve. This helps remove any initial clumps in the powder. Pour in the hot water and use a bamboo matcha whisk to make M-shape movements for 30 to 40 seconds, until the matcha is nice and frothy with no clumps remaining.

2. To make an iced latte, fill a glass with ice and add the plant milk and, if using, the vanilla and maple syrup. Pour the whisked matcha into the glass, stir, and enjoy. To serve hot, heat up or steam your plant milk of choice and combine with the vanilla, if using. Stir the matcha into the milk and enjoy.

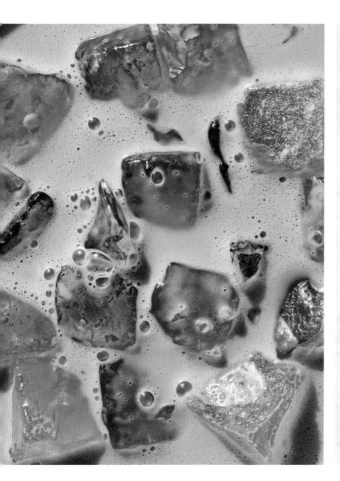

pistachio milk matcha with cheesecake cream

If you frequent a bubble tea shop, there's a good chance you'll find something called cheese tea on the menu. I'd thought the trend would never make its way out of Asia, but then I noticed cheese tea starting to pop up on the menus in New York City and L.A. In theory, the cheese and dessert combo isn't that crazy at all. Although I'm not sure I'll ever be ready for a gouda latte, a cheesecake cream–topped matcha latte is a mild take that I'm totally down with, and I think you'll love it, too!

MAKES 1 SERVING

2 tablespoons vegan cream cheese, homemade (page 18) or store-bought, softened

1 teaspoon freshly squeezed lemon juice

1 teaspoon pure maple syrup, plus more to taste

½ teaspoon vanilla bean paste

Pinch of kosher salt

Plant milk of your choice, to blend

Everyday Matcha Latte (page 124), made with pistachio milk

1. In a small bowl, whisk together the cream cheese, lemon juice, maple syrup, vanilla bean paste, and salt. Adjust sweetness as needed, then whisk in the plant milk, teaspoon by teaspoon, until you have a smooth and spreadable consistency.

2. Top the latte with the cheesecake cream and stir before enjoying.

raspberry
cheesecake
smoothie,
page 130

key lime
smoothie,
page 133

black sesame
cacao smoothie,
page 131

raspberry cheesecake smoothie

Something about the combination of cashews, lemon juice, and fruit produces the most incredible cheesecake-like flavor, so I've named this the Raspberry Cheesecake Smoothie! It's a creamy, tangy, very pink drink that you'll love. Try adding a vanilla plant protein powder to make a post-workout smoothie.

MAKES 1 LARGE OR 2 SMALL SERVINGS

¾ cup frozen raspberries

1 very ripe banana, peeled and frozen

⅓ cup raw cashews, soaked in water for at least 3 hours or preferably overnight

2 teaspoons freshly squeezed lemon juice

1 teaspoon vanilla bean paste or pure vanilla extract

1 cup plant milk of your choice, plus more as needed

Combine all the ingredients in a blender and blend until smooth. Add the amount of plant milk to achieve a texture that's to your liking. For a thinner smoothie, add more milk. For a thicker smoothie or to turn this into a smoothie bowl with a spoonable texture, start with less than 1 cup milk.

black sesame cacao smoothie

Black sesame is often considered savory in flavor, but it really lends itself nicely to desserts. It actually tastes a little bit like cookies and cream to me! Around the Lunar New Year, my family often enjoys black sesame–filled glutinous rice dumplings, and I was convinced they were filled with crushed Oreo cookies for the longest time. This smoothie taps into the power of black sesame.

MAKES 1 SERVING

¼ cup black sesame seeds, plus more for optional topping

1 large banana, peeled and frozen

¾ cup plant milk of your choice, plus more as needed

1 teaspoon vanilla bean paste

1 tablespoon cacao powder

1 teaspoon pure maple syrup, optional

1 tablespoon toasted coconut flakes, for topping

1. Toast the sesame seeds in a small dry pan over low heat, stirring constantly, for 2 to 3 minutes, until fragrant. Transfer to a plate to keep them from burning.

2. Combine the toasted sesame seeds, banana, plant milk, vanilla bean paste, cacao powder, and maple syrup (if using) in a high-powered blender. Blend until completely smooth, adding more plant milk as needed to reach the desired thickness.

3. Pour into a tall glass and top with the toasted coconut flakes and additional toasted sesame seeds, if desired. Enjoy immediately.

key lime smoothie

Disclaimer: There are no Key limes in this smoothie. But it's a good thing, because conventional limes are much easier to find year-round. This smoothie is reminiscent of classic Key lime pie, except you can enjoy it for breakfast and it's packed with nutrients to power your day.

MAKES 1 SERVING

1 large ripe banana, peeled and frozen

½ cup full-fat coconut milk, plus more as needed

¼ cup freshly squeezed lime juice, plus optional grated zest for garnish

2 to 3 teaspoons pure maple syrup, to taste

2 teaspoons pure vanilla extract or vanilla bean paste

1 teaspoon ceremonial-grade matcha powder, for color, optional

¼ cup rolled oats, for a thicker consistency, optional

Dairy-free yogurt, for garnish, optional

1. Chilled a tall glass in the freezer while you prepare the drink.

3. Blend the banana, coconut milk, lime juice, maple syrup, vanilla, matcha powder, and rolled oats (if using) in a high-powered blender until smooth.

3. When the smoothie is ready to serve, drizzle the yogurt on the inner walls of the chilled glass to create patterns, if you like. Pour the smoothie into the glass and serve with fresh lime zest on top, if desired.

shanghai sunrise (mocktail)

When I lived in Shanghai, I often ordered a tequila sunrise whenever I was at a bar or club, but the drink never seemed to come the same way twice at the cheap sports bars and questionable clubs I frequented. So I'm taking liberties as well! This is my version of the drink, minus the alcohol and hangover. If you want to get really fancy, throw in an ounce or two of a nonalcoholic tequila alternative.

MAKES 1 SERVING

5 ounces (½ cup plus 2 tablespoons) orange juice, freshly squeezed or store-bought

½ ounce (1 tablespoon) freshly squeezed lime juice

1 to 2 ounces (2 to 4 tablespoons) nonalcoholic tequila alternative, optional

Ice

Sparkling water, to top

1 ounce (2 tablespoons) grenadine syrup

Maraschino cherries (I like the dye-free Amarena Fabbri and Tillen Farms brands), for garnish, optional

1 or 2 orange slices, for garnish, optional

1. In a cocktail shaker or glass jar with a lid, combine the orange juice, lime juice, and tequila alternative (if using). Shake vigorously. Add ice to the shaker and shake again.

2. Strain into a tall glass with ice, then top off with sparkling water. Gently pour in the grenadine over the back of a spoon to layer it on top. Serve with maraschino cherries and fresh orange slices, if desired.

sesame, soy, spice

garden gimlet (chamomile and citrus mocktail)

A classic gimlet is made with vodka or gin, lime juice, and simple syrup. This take is heavy on the citrus with a touch of garden thanks to a chamomile-infused simple syrup. Not only is it floral, but it also has a calming effect and can promote relaxation and rest. Think bedtime tea, but a little more fun and a lot more delicious. You can opt to add in an ounce or two of zero-proof vodka or gin if you'd like, for a more authentic taste.

MAKES 1 SERVING

Ice

Juice of 1 lime, plus 1 lime slice for garnish

Juice of 1 lemon

Juice of 1 small grapefruit

1 to 2 teaspoons Coconut Sugar Simple Syrup (page 123), made with chamomile, or to taste

2 ounces nonalcoholic vodka or gin alternative, optional

Sparkling water

Fresh chamomile flowers, for garnish

Place ice in a cocktail shaker or glass jar with a lid. Pour in the lime juice, lemon juice, grapefruit juice, chamomile syrup, and zero-proof vodka or gin (if using) and vigorously shake to combine. Strain into a glass with fresh ice, top off with sparkling water, and garnish with fresh chamomile flowers and a slice of lime, if you like.

5 **long life noodles, rice, and other mains**

My grandpa on my mother's side, who we call Jichang—pronounced *jee-chang* and which came about because at a young age I couldn't fully pronounce *ojī-san*, Japanese for "grandpa"— has always been a man of routine. He worked in Flushing, Queens, home to New York's largest Chinatown, where the crosswalks are always bustling, most awnings feature Chinese characters, you can get by without speaking any English, and the streets are lined with fishmongers and vegetable and fruit stands.

Before my family's first move overseas to Taiwan, I remember Jichang coming home most nights with a plastic bag so heavy the handles looked like they were cutting off the circulation in his fingers. Some nights, the bag was full of live crabs. Other nights it was lobster or fresh fish. He parked his car in the garage, entered through the back door, took his shoes off, and handed the bag off to my grandma, who transferred the contents into the sink. I always studied the outline of the bag and tried to guess its contents. Jichang, like many Asian American immigrants, is a fairly frugal man in most areas of his life. He scoffs at conventional grocery store prices, always remarking that things are "too expensive," and loves nothing more than a good deal. But when it comes to food, he enjoys true luxury—the decadent, rich, and high-ticket foods. Think bone marrow, oysters, sea urchin sushi, crab, lobster, bottarga, and, of course, steak. These were not foods he grew up with. Jichang grew up eating primarily vegetables, hailing from a

farmer family in Taiwan. But after his move to the United States and his eventual success, he was able to afford the finer things and loved to share them with us.

When I first became vegan, Jichang was always horrified watching me eat dinner. I would skip the main attraction, his Flushing special of the day, and instead eat the vegetable sides and the rice. One day he asked me, "Why are you only eating the commoner's food!? What about the fish!? How can you survive?" Jichang considers noodles, rice, vegetables, and most grains "commoner's food." It sounds a lot more classist than I think he intends, English not being his first language, but it's only half joking. It took a while for me to realize what the contents of the double-, sometimes triple-lined *THANK YOU HAVE A NICE DAY* bag meant to him. It wasn't so much about nutrition or my well-being, but more about his desire to share with his loved ones the food he worked so hard for. I usually responded with an eye roll and the reminder that I was still, in fact, alive. As time passed, I started making it a point to remind him how many years it had been since I had gone vegan. "Jichang, it has already been *eight years*, see!" Although Korean barbecue continues to rise in popularity and Japanese food is commonly thought of as raw fish, most people in East Asian countries historically subsisted primarily on plants. In college I took a food history class, where we studied the evolution of food and the various factors and circumstances that have influenced changes in food choice and trends. One of the best mandatory reading assignments was *The China Study: The Most Comprehensive Study of Nutrition Ever Conducted* by T. Colin Campbell and Thomas M. Campbell II. I was surprised to learn that rice, vegetables, and grains were the foundation of most meals for the wide majority of Asian countries. This old Chinese proverb also hints at primarily plant-based sustenance:

Fish brings heat, meat brings phlegm, but vegetables and tofu keep you well.
魚生火，肉生痰，青菜豆腐保平安. (Yú shēnghuǒ, ròu shēng tán, q ngcài dòufu bǎo píng'ān.)

Meat was considered a privilege because, back in the day, only the affluent could afford it, and it thus became a sort of status symbol. Meat has now become much more integrated into the modern diet, even in Asian countries, but especially among my grandfather's generation, it continues to be an aspirational addition to the plate. Jichang wasn't quite as excited by this revelation, but he was more understanding when I mentioned shojin food and Buddhist mock meats. Interestingly, despite some of my family's ill perceptions about veganism, in all of my three cultures there are groups of people who eat a primarily vegan diet. In Korea, temple food consumed by Buddhist monks and nuns excludes meat from the diet as it is believed to "extinguish the seeds of compassion." Similarly, *shojin ryori*, Buddhist vegetarian cuisine, does not include animal byproducts in the name of the value of *ahimsa*, or compassion and nonviolence. Finally, in Taiwan and China, religions that emphasize less meat consumption, like Buddhism, Confucianism, and Taoism, are commonly observed, so faux meat is easy to find. Everything from mock duck to mock chicken drumsticks to mock fish can be found at markets and in restaurants. I wouldn't call myself Buddhist by any means, but for now I've found that referring to my plate of vegetables as "shojin-style food" makes it easier for Jichang to understand. I once felt guilty for stripping him of the opportunity to share his hard-earned seafood with me, but now he has instead focused his attention on premium vegetables. He'll bring me bags of pea shoots, my favorite vegetable, and meatless *zongzi* (glutinous sticky rice) chock-full of peanuts (the good stuff, according to him). The best part is that I can joke with him that buying vegetables instead of meat is always a good deal.

mum's macrobiotic bowl

Macrobiotic eating originated in Japan, and the idea behind it is to promote longevity and health through a balance of types of foods. Followers of a macrobiotic diet believe in foods being "hot" and "cold," or rather *yin* and *yang*, as well as acidic and alkaline. A macrobiotic bowl represents an ideal balance of all of these elements. There's typically a strong emphasis on grains, vegetables, and fermented foods. The best part of macrobiotic bowls is they're easy to put together and you can save even more time by using pre-prepped components. Grains or cereals make up the base of a basic macrobiotic bowl, accounting for 40 to 50 percent of it, followed by vegetables, which make up another 25 percent, then lentils or legumes, seaweed, and finally fermented foods. Between my dad's Korean heritage and my mum's Japanese heritage, we ate a lot of macrobiotic bowls for dinner that were something in between bibimbap (the Korean mixed rice bowl with a spicy red pepper sauce and vegetables sautéed in toasted sesame oil) and donburi (the Japanese rice bowl that usually features a simmered protein or veggie over rice). It was such an easy dish to lay out on the table, really customizable, and something we loved. In my first year in college, I shared a meal with a friend at Souen, a Japanese spot in SoHo, and seeing their macrobiotic bowl on the menu was so comforting. I took a photo and sent it to my parents and continued to eat there at least once a month, despite the trek on the 1 train that it required. This dish is a humble, balanced, and homey bowl, best enjoyed with in-season veg and your favorite sauce or dressing.

MAKES 1 LARGE SERVING

long life noodles, rice, and other mains

1 cup chopped kale, steamed

⅓ cup steamed broccoli florets

1 teaspoon toasted sesame oil

½ teaspoon kosher salt

1 cup cooked brown rice or other rice of your choice

½ cup thickly sliced kabocha squash or sweet potato, steamed

½ cup cooked shelled edamame beans or other bean of your choice

¼ cup Sunomono cucumber salad (page 54)

Miso Tahini Dressing (page 78), to taste

1 teaspoon toasted sesame seeds, for garnish, optional

1. Massage the steamed kale and broccoli with the toasted sesame oil and salt and set aside.

2. Assemble the macrobiotic bowl or plate starting with the brown rice, then arrange the kale, broccoli, squash, beans, and cucumber salad on top.

3. Drizzle with the dressing and toss to incorporate. Garnish with toasted sesame seeds, if you like, before digging in.

mushroom and walnut crumble

Many Asian dishes feature some kind of ground meat on top, so this meaty mushroom and walnut-based crumble is my go-to when I want to re-create such a dish and make it a little more convincing. I also use it in other dishes in place of ground beef or meat! It's delicious tossed with Section 7 Noodles (page 149) or piled on top of Cucumber Sesame Noodles (page 146).

MAKES ABOUT 3 CUPS, FOR 4 TO 5 SERVINGS

¾ cup walnuts, soaked in hot water for 30 minutes and drained

10 ounces fresh shiitake mushrooms

2 tablespoons neutral oil (see page xvi)

3 scallions, thinly sliced

1½ teaspoons finely grated garlic

One ½-inch piece fresh ginger, peeled and finely grated

2 to 3 tablespoons tamari, to taste

2 teaspoons toasted sesame oil

Kosher salt, to taste

Freshly ground black pepper, to taste

1. Combine the walnuts and mushrooms in a food processor and gently pulse a few times. Be sure not to pulse too finely as you want a ground beef–like texture.

2. Heat the oil in a large pan over medium-high heat. Add the scallions, garlic, and ginger and sauté for a minute, until nice and fragrant. Add the mushroom and walnut mixture and cook for 7 to 8 minutes, until fragrant and tender, stirring occasionally, then cook undisturbed for a minute or so to develop a little bit of a crust on some of the edges. Add the tamari and sesame oil and season with salt and pepper. Toss and cook for another 30 seconds to combine.

cucumber sesame noodles

8 ounces gluten-free noodles of your choice

Neutral oil (see page xvi), to prevent sticking

¼ cup Chinese sesame paste (see page xvii) or sesame peanut paste

½ teaspoon toasted sesame oil

3 tablespoons rice wine vinegar

2 tablespoons tamari

1 teaspoon pure maple syrup

2 garlic cloves, finely minced

1 teaspoon red chili flakes, optional

Warm water, as needed for consistency

1 or 2 Persian cucumbers, julienned

¼ cup crushed roasted peanuts

2 scallions, green tops only, sliced diagonally

2 teaspoons toasted sesame seeds

Everything Bagel Chili Crisp (page 192)

Mushroom and Walnut Crumble (page 145), for serving, optional

Sesame noodles were popularized in the 1970s, thanks to Shorty Tang and his New York City restaurant, Hwa Yuan. How I ended up consuming 12NT (about $1.76) bowls of this dish multiple times a week in Taiwan is a mystery to me. Sesame noodles and fresh cucumber on top of noodle dishes are not rare in Taiwan, and you can absolutely find the dish all over the city! I love the recipe because it comes together in 10 minutes and feels like a representation of my first move overseas—a mix of something New York and something Taiwan.

MAKES 2 SERVINGS

1. Prepare the noodles according to the package directions. Strain and toss with a little bit of neutral oil to help prevent sticking while you prepare the sauce.

2. In a medium bowl, whisk together the sesame paste, sesame oil, vinegar, tamari, maple syrup, garlic, and chili flakes, if using. Add warm water by the tablespoon and whisk after each addition until you achieve a nice consistency (the mixture should be pourable but still creamy and rich).

3. To assemble, add the noodles to the bowl and toss them to coat, then divide them between two bowls. Top with the cucumbers, roasted peanuts, scallions, sesame seeds, and chili crisp to taste. You can also serve with Mushroom and Walnut Crumble on top!

section 7 noodles

If you asked me what my favorite recipes were when I was growing up, this would be high on the list. Named after a neighborhood in Taipei, it was one of the first Taiwanese dishes I really enjoyed after our move there, and I'd order it whenever we ate out. Seeing it on the menu always gave me a sense of security, knowing there was something I'd enjoy (and that was cilantro-free). We ate this often, both out and at home—but of course my mum's recipe came with no formal measurements.

MAKES 4 SERVINGS

5 dried shiitake mushrooms

8 ounces bifun ("rice stick") noodles

3 tablespoons neutral oil (see page xvi)

2 carrots, peeled and julienned

½ white onion, thinly sliced

1 garlic clove, minced

4 napa cabbage leaves, thinly sliced

¼ cup tamari

¼ cup rice wine

1 teaspoon ground white pepper

Mushroom and Walnut Crumble (page 145)

1. Soak the mushrooms in room-temperature water for about 15 minutes, until tender, then drain and reserve the liquid for later. Remove and discard the mushroom stems, then thinly slice the mushrooms and set aside.

2. Meanwhile, soak the noodles in a bowl of cold water for 10 minutes, until tender. Drain and set aside.

3. In a large skillet, heat 1 tablespoon of the oil over medium-high heat. Add the carrots and onion and sauté for 2 minutes, until tender. Add the garlic and sauté for another 30 seconds. Add the remaining 2 tablespoons oil, the cabbage, and the sliced shiitakes and sauté for 3 to 5 minutes, until the veggies get a nice char. Add the tamari, rice wine, white pepper, and ¼ cup of the mushroom soaking liquid and toss to coat. Add the noodles and mushroom-walnut crumble, toss to coat, and serve.

shiitake veggie burgers

In a world where Impossible Burger and Beyond Meat patties aim to replicate meat as closely as possible, I am personally drawn to more straightforward vegetable burgers. In my opinion, if you're able to make a delicious patty out of vegetables, then you really know how to cook. This burger has a long ingredient list, but the preparation is almost meditative, and you'll end up with many patties to freeze for later. Serve with fresh tomato slices, lettuce, red onion, pickles, a bun, and any other desired toppings.

To freeze the uncooked patties, arrange them on a nonstick sheet pan, making sure they don't touch. Freeze overnight, then transfer them to an airtight container of your choice, placing a small piece of parchment paper between each patty to keep them from sticking together. Store in the freezer for up to 2 months.

MAKES 12 TO 15 PATTIES

1 small or ½ large eggplant

Neutral oil (see page xvi)

Kosher salt

1 medium yellow onion, roughly chopped

1 leek, halved, cleaned well, and roughly chopped

1 celery stalk, roughly chopped

1 large carrot, peeled and roughly chopped

2 tablespoons double-concentrated tomato paste

¾ cup (half a 15.5-ounce can) chickpeas, drained

½ cup roughly chopped roasted cashews

¼ cup buckwheat groats, cooked

1. Preheat the oven to 350°F.

2. To roast the eggplant, cut it in half lengthwise, coat lightly all over with oil, and season with ½ teaspoon salt. Place cut side down on a sheet pan and roast for 25 minutes, until soft. Scoop out the flesh and discard the skin.

3. Pour enough oil into a large skillet or heavy-bottomed pot to lightly cover the bottom. Heat over medium-high heat, then add the onion, leek, celery, and carrot and sauté until soft, 5 to 8 minutes. Add the tomato paste and cook, stirring often, until it turns a deep red color. Remove the vegetables and set aside; reserve the skillet.

4. Pulse the chickpeas in a food processor until roughly chopped and transfer to a large bowl.

5. In the food processor, purée the roasted eggplant. Add it to the bowl with the chickpeas, along with the cashews and buckwheat.

½ pound shiitake mushrooms, sliced

½ pound cremini mushrooms, sliced

⅓ cup potato starch or cornstarch

2 tablespoons nutritional yeast

1 tablespoon white miso paste

1 tablespoon tamari

1 teaspoon ground cumin

1 teaspoon garlic powder

½ teaspoon smoked paprika

⅛ teaspoon liquid smoke

Freshly ground black pepper, to taste

4 cups gluten-free cornflake cereal, finely ground in the food processor to a sandy texture, or gluten-free panko bread crumbs

6. In the pan used for the vegetables, add enough oil to lightly cover the bottom and heat over medium-high heat. Add the mushrooms and cook, without stirring, until tender with slightly golden-brown edges, 5 to 8 minutes. Transfer the mushrooms and sautéed vegetables to the food processor and pulse into a chunky mixture. Be sure not to process too finely.

7. Add the mushroom mixture to the bowl with the chickpeas, along with the potato starch, nutritional yeast, miso paste, tamari, cumin, garlic powder, paprika, liquid smoke, 1 teaspoon salt, and the pepper and use a spatula to mix everything well. Place the mixture in the fridge for at least 30 minutes, or until cool enough to work with your hands.

8. To form the veggie patties, spread the cornflake crumbs in a shallow dish. Scoop out ½ cup of the mixture and roll it into a ball. Coat the ball with crumbs and gently press down on the ball to flatten it to about 1 inch thick. Repeat to form and coat the rest of the patties.

9. Heat 2 to 3 tablespoons neutral oil in a large skillet over medium heat. Working in batches as needed, add the patties, making sure they aren't touching. Cook for 3 to 4 minutes per side, turning gently with a spatula, until golden brown.

long life noodles, rice, and other mains

shredded korean bbq bulgogi tofu

Bulgogi is an iconic Korean meat dish that, when I was young, I'd often eat with a bowl of rice and call it a meal. In place of beef, this recipe calls for shredded tofu that's baked, then sautéed in a pan. This technique gives the tofu a meaty texture with crisp edges, and a standard bulgogi sauce makes it irresistible.

MAKES 3 TO 4 SERVINGS

TOFU

One 15-ounce package high-protein tofu (see page xvii)

1 tablespoon neutral oil (see page xvi)

2 teaspoons toasted sesame oil

2 teaspoons kosher salt

SAUCE

½ Asian pear, peeled and finely grated

3 garlic cloves, minced

1 teaspoon grated fresh ginger

¼ cup tamari

2 tablespoons water

2 tablespoons rice wine

2 tablespoons coconut sugar

2 teaspoons toasted sesame oil

1 teaspoon gochugaru

GARNISH

Sesame seeds

Thinly sliced scallion greens

1. Preheat the oven to 350°F and line a sheet pan with parchment paper or a nonstick baking mat.

2. To prepare the tofu, wrap in a kitchen towel and press gently to remove any excess moisture. Cut into two pieces so it's easier to handle, then shred using a cheese grater, just as you would a block of cheese. Transfer the shredded tofu to a large bowl and toss with the neutral oil, sesame oil, and salt. Spread the tofu out evenly on the prepared sheet pan and bake for 20 minutes, tossing halfway through. This step will help dry it out a bit.

3. Meanwhile, to prepare the sauce, combine the sauce ingredients in a medium bowl and whisk until smooth.

4. In a medium pan over medium heat, combine the sauce and tofu. Bring to a simmer and cook until the sauce reduces and is absorbed by the tofu, 5 to 8 minutes, tossing with a spatula occasionally. Garnish with the sesame seeds and scallion greens and serve.

japanese cashew curry

8 tablespoons (1 stick) vegan butter

¼ cup gluten-free flour (see page xv)

3 tablespoons S&B curry powder (see page xvii)

1 tablespoon nutritional yeast

1 teaspoon ground coriander

1 teaspoon ground cumin

2 tablespoons unsweetened cashew butter

1 tablespoon neutral oil (see page xvi)

2 shallots, thinly sliced

2 garlic cloves, minced

½ teaspoon kosher salt

2 large carrots, peeled and cut into rustic chunks

1 large russet potato, cut into rustic chunks

½ yellow onion, roughly chopped

5 cups vegetable broth

⅓ cup tamari

2 tablespoons coconut sugar

Some like Japanese curry with *fukujinzuke* (a pickled condiment), some like it as a sauce for udon, and my aunt Ohmi likes hers with *just a little bit* of rice. Japanese curry differs from Indian curries in that the flavor profile is more mellow and almost a little sweet. It's also thickened with roux so the texture is heartier, too. Instead of a heavy presence of just one or two primary spices, Japanese curry tends to feature an almost equal blend of every spice ingredient. You can find roux cubes at the store (and in almost any Japanese family kitchen), but this roux is gluten-free friendly and easy to make at home.

MAKES 3 TO 4 SERVINGS

1. Melt the butter in a large pot over medium heat. Add the flour, curry powder, nutritional yeast, coriander, cumin, and cashew butter. Combine over the heat, whisking constantly to create a roux, 3 to 5 minutes. Transfer to a small bowl and set aside.

2. Pour the oil into the same pot over medium heat, add the shallots, garlic, and salt, and sauté until soft and fragrant, 3 to 4 minutes. Add the carrots, potato, and onion and sauté for 2 to 3 minutes, just until fragrant. Add the vegetable broth and bring the mixture to a boil. Cook until the vegetables are fork tender. Cook time will vary based on the size of your veggies.

3. Add the roux to the pot and stir to incorporate. Lower the heat to a simmer and add the tamari and coconut sugar. Cook for 5 to 8 minutes, until the curry has thickened and resembles a gravy. Serve with rice.

long life noodles, rice, and other mains

creamy pea soup with crunchy pea croutons

A springy green soup complete with pea croutons! This is a gorgeous soup and one for the pea lovers.

MAKES 2 SERVINGS

CRUNCHY PEA CROUTONS

⅓ cup peas, fresh or thawed frozen

1½ teaspoons neutral oil (see page xvi)

2 tablespoons nutritional yeast

1 teaspoon kosher salt

½ teaspoon garlic powder

½ teaspoon onion powder

SOUP

2 tablespoons neutral oil (see page xvi)

1 small yellow onion, thinly sliced

3 garlic cloves, minced

½ teaspoon kosher salt

3 cups peas, fresh or thawed frozen

3 cups vegetable broth

¼ cup unsweetened plant milk of your choice

1 teaspoon white miso paste

Freshly ground black pepper, to taste

Extra virgin olive oil, for serving

1. Preheat the oven to 400°F.

2. To make the crunchy pea croutons, toss the peas with the oil in a medium bowl. Add the nutritional yeast, salt, garlic powder, and onion powder and toss again to coat. Spread the peas on a rimmed sheet pan and bake for 12 to 15 minutes, until slightly crunchy.

3. To make the soup, heat the neutral oil in a medium pot over medium heat. Add the onion and sauté for 2 to 3 minutes, until tender. Add the garlic and salt and cook for another 2 minutes, until fragrant. Add the peas and sauté for just a minute, until vibrant green. Add the broth, bring the mixture to a boil, and then lower the heat to a simmer. Cook for 10 minutes, until the peas are tender.

4. Transfer the mixture to a blender, making sure there's an opening for steam release, along with the plant milk and miso paste. Blend until completely smooth.

5. Divide the soup among bowls and top with pea croutons. Season with pepper and a drizzle of extra virgin olive oil.

spring pasta,
page 160

summer pasta,
page 161

fall pasta,
page 162

winter pasta,
page 163

pasta all year

My formula for lazy pasta goes something like this: an allium (such as onion, garlic, shallot, leek, and/or scallion), two in-season veggies, a fresh herb (like dill, mint, basil, thyme, oregano, or rosemary), olive oil, and finishing touches (like chili flakes, crunchy nuts, or seeds and citrus). It works year-round and really lets the produce of the season shine. Following that basic playbook, here are four recipes, one for each of the four seasons.

EACH RECIPE MAKES 2 SERVINGS

spring pasta

Kosher salt

6 ounces gluten-free pasta of your choice

2 tablespoons olive oil, plus more as needed

½ teaspoon red chili flakes

1 cup roughly chopped sugar snap peas

1 leek, white part only, halved, cleaned well, and thinly sliced (about 1 cup)

4 garlic cloves, thinly sliced

5 kale leaves, stemmed and roughly chopped

Juice of ½ lemon, plus grated zest for garnish

Freshly ground black pepper

1. Bring 6 cups of water to a boil in a large pot. Add 2 heavy pinches of salt and the pasta and cook according to the package directions until al dente. Drain, reserving about ¼ cup of the pasta water, and set aside.

2. In a medium saucepan over medium heat, heat the olive oil. Add the chili flakes and snap peas and cook, undisturbed, for about a minute to achieve a nice char. Toss and sauté for another minute or so, until the snap peas are lightly charred on all sides. Add the leek and cook until aromatic and tender, 3 to 5 minutes. Add 1 teaspoon salt, the garlic, and kale and sauté for another minute or so, until the garlic is tender and the kale is wilted.

3. Add the cooked pasta to the pan, along with the reserved pasta water, and toss. Add the lemon juice and salt and pepper to taste. Finish with lemon zest to taste and serve.

summer pasta

Kosher salt

6 ounces gluten-free pasta of your choice

2 tablespoons olive oil, plus more as needed

½ teaspoon red chili flakes

1 cup corn kernels, fresh or thawed frozen

1 yellow squash, cut into quarters lengthwise and thinly sliced

4 garlic cloves, thinly sliced

Freshly ground black pepper

Handful of fresh basil leaves, torn, for garnish

Vegan Ricotta Cheese (page 179), to taste

1. Bring 6 cups of water to a boil in a large pot. Add 2 heavy pinches of salt and the pasta and cook according to the package directions until al dente. Drain, reserving about ¼ cup of the pasta water, and set aside.

2. In a medium saucepan over medium heat, heat the olive oil. Add the chili flakes, corn, and squash and let sit, undisturbed, for about a minute to achieve a nice char. Toss and sauté for another minute or so, until tender. Add the garlic and salt and pepper to taste and sauté for another 3 minutes or so, until the garlic is fragrant.

3. Add the cooked pasta to the pan, along with the reserved pasta water, and toss. Finish with freshly torn basil and vegan ricotta as desired.

fall pasta

Kosher salt

6 ounces gluten-free pasta of your choice

2 tablespoons olive oil, plus more as needed

1 cup finely diced peeled butternut squash

1 cup roughly chopped mushrooms of your choice (I like to use maitake)

2 fresh thyme sprigs

1 teaspoon finely chopped fresh rosemary leaves

4 garlic cloves, thinly sliced

Freshly ground black pepper, to taste

Splash of oat milk, optional

Nutritional yeast, to taste

1. Bring 6 cups of water to a boil in a large pot. Add 2 heavy pinches of salt and the pasta and cook according to the package directions until al dente. Drain, reserving about ¼ cup of the pasta water, and set aside.

2. In a large saucepan or skillet over medium heat, heat the olive oil. Add the butternut squash, season with a pinch of salt, and cook, turning the cubes with a spatula, until nicely golden brown on all sides, 5 to 8 minutes. Remove from the pan and set aside.

3. In the same pan, add a touch of olive oil if needed and the mushrooms. Cook undisturbed for 5 to 6 minutes, until slightly golden brown around the edges. Add the thyme, rosemary, and garlic and sauté for 2 to 3 minutes, until aromatic. Season with salt and pepper.

4. Add the cooked pasta and butternut squash to the pan, along with the reserved pasta water, and toss to coat. Remove the thyme sprigs and finish with a touch of oat milk for a creamy feel, if desired. Garnish with nutritional yeast and season with salt and pepper.

winter pasta

Kosher salt

6 ounces pasta of your choice

2 tablespoons olive oil, plus more as needed

½ pound Brussels sprouts, trimmed and thinly sliced

5 garlic cloves, thinly sliced

Red chili flakes, to taste

½ cup roasted shelled pistachios

Juice of ½ lemon, plus grated zest for garnish

Freshly ground black pepper

1. Bring 6 cups of water to a boil in a large pot. Add 2 heavy pinches of salt and the pasta and cook according to the package directions until al dente. Drain, reserving about ¼ cup of the pasta water, and set aside.

2. In a medium saucepan over medium heat, heat the olive oil. Add the Brussels sprouts, season with a pinch of salt, and cook undisturbed for a few minutes to allow for a little char to develop before tossing to sauté. Add the garlic, chili flakes, and pistachios and sauté for 1 or 2 minutes, until fragrant.

3. Add the cooked pasta to the pan, along with the reserved pasta water, and toss to coat. Finish with the lemon juice and salt and pepper to taste, along with lemon zest.

curried kabocha squash soup

Curried pumpkin soup is a classic, but this version uses kabocha, a squash we eat often in Japan, and S&B curry powder, which has a distinct flavor of its own. This soup is creamy, rich, warming, and so easy to make.

MAKES 2 TO 3 SERVINGS

2 tablespoons olive oil or neutral oil (see page xvi), plus 2 teaspoons if making the optional garnish

1 large leek, halved, cleaned well, and finely sliced (optional: reserve ¼ cup for a garnish)

3 garlic cloves, minced

1 tablespoon S&B curry powder (see page xvii)

½ teaspoon red chili flakes

2 cups finely diced peeled kabocha squash

½ teaspoon smoked paprika

5 cups vegetable broth

1 teaspoon tamari

½ teaspoon kosher salt, plus more for the optional garnish

Ground white pepper, to taste

1. Heat the olive oil in a large pot over medium heat. Add the leek and sauté until soft and fragrant, 2 to 3 minutes. Add the garlic, curry powder, and chili flakes and cook for another minute, until the garlic and spices are fragrant. Add the squash and paprika and cook for 2 to 3 minutes to bloom the spices and coat the squash, then add the vegetable broth. Bring the mixture to a low boil, cover, and cook for about 7 minutes, until the squash is fork tender.

2. Add the tamari, then transfer the contents of the pot to a high-powered blender (or use an immersion blender right in the pot), and blend until completely smooth. (Take care not to overfill the blender; work in batches as needed!) Season with the salt and white pepper.

3. To make the optional leek garnish, heat 2 teaspoons olive oil in a small skillet and add the ¼ cup leeks and a touch of salt. Sauté until the leeks are tender and lightly golden in color, 5 or 6 minutes.

4. Serve the soup, garnished with the leeks, if desired.

spicy peanut ramen

1 bok choy head, trimmed and halved lengthwise

2 tablespoons neutral oil (see page xvi), plus more as needed

2 ounces oyster mushrooms, roughly torn

2 ounces shiitake mushrooms, thinly sliced

Kosher salt

1 teaspoon toasted sesame oil

2 tablespoons red miso paste

2 tablespoons gochujang

1 tablespoon creamy unsweetened peanut butter

3 cups vegetable broth

3 scallions, white parts only, thinly sliced, plus 1 thinly sliced for garnish

2 garlic cloves, minced

1 cup unsweetened soymilk, homemade (page 116) or store-bought

1 to 2 tablespoons tamari, or to taste

1 serving ramen noodles or rice noodles, cooked according to the package directions (without the seasoning packet, if any)

2 tablespoons roughly chopped roasted peanuts

½ teaspoon toasted white sesame seeds

Instant ramen is a true comfort food in any Asian household, and this homemade version is not only completely plant based but also really rich in flavor. It's *allll* about the broth and, thanks to mushrooms, miso, tamari, and peanuts, it does not disappoint.

MAKES 2 SERVINGS

1. Bring a small pot of water to a boil over medium heat. Add the bok choy and cook for 1 minute. Remove from the pot and immediately rinse under cool water. Drain and set aside.

2. Heat the oil in a medium pot over medium heat. Add all the mushrooms and a touch of salt and cook until rich in color and cooked through, not stirring too often, 3 to 5 minutes. Add the sesame oil and sauté for another minute, shaking the pan or tossing with a spatula. Remove the mushrooms and set aside; reserve the pot.

3. In a small bowl, whisk together the miso paste, gochujang, peanut butter, and enough vegetable broth to be able to whisk the mixture into a pourable sauce.

4. Add the scallion white parts and garlic to the medium pot, along with enough oil to coat the bottom, plus a pinch of salt. Sauté for 2 minutes over medium-low heat, until fragrant. Add the peanut butter–miso mixture, the remaining vegetable broth, and the soymilk and bring to a boil. Lower the heat to a simmer, cover, and cook for 10 to 12 minutes, until the broth reduces by about a quarter. Stir in the tamari.

5. To serve, divide the noodles between two bowls, pour the broth over the noodles, and top with the bok choy, mushrooms, roasted peanuts, toasted sesame seeds, and sliced scallion.

oncle's onion
pizza, page 176

6 more things my family members, who never measure anything, like to make

I have always loved watching Obā-chan cook. In my earlier years, I would watch as she pulled glossy buckwheat noodles out of a pot or cooked lotus root, never measuring but somehow always knowing exactly how much of each seasoning to add to the pan.

I was obsessed with food, but mostly because I wasn't really eating enough of it. Obā-chan's dishes would make it to the table and I'd pull out my Tupperware salad. I felt like a voyeur, allowing myself to smell the sizzling garlic and watching enviously as my sister Chloe and uncle Eugene slurped their spaghetti up with chopsticks but never taking a bite myself.

"You're looking really thin!"

"You've gained some weight, ah?"

"You need to eat more! Come, eat!"

It didn't help that talking about food and weight, even while eating a meal, is considered normal in Asian culture. No matter what direction I was headed on the scale, I felt like Goldilocks trying to find the perfect size and number to stick to. If you're too thin, you need to *eat more*; but if you're gaining weight, Asian family members will let you know—then proceed to encourage you to eat the food they've prepared for you.

After healing my relationship with food and being a few years into my vegan lifestyle, I became even more fascinated with Obā-chan's cooking, but this time I wanted to learn how to replicate her dishes. Whereas I was once hyper-focused on the numbers and macros of any food I consumed, through recovery I was able to rediscover a love for

food itself. In addition, I had been cooking vegan long enough that I no longer felt the need to stick to my arsenal of vegan recipes I had bookmarked (like lentil Bolognese and vegan broccoli cheddar soup). I was ready to take a stab at replicating my favorite cultural dishes with plant-based ingredients.

As Obā-chan made *zenzai* (red bean soup), I took notes and asked her for the recipe—only to be given sparse instructions with zero measurements. Obā-chan never really measured; she could make most of the recipes with her eyes closed. I watched carefully and tried to weigh out ingredients in the various bowls and cups she'd use to "measure," in an attempt to transcribe her recipes, but they always required a little tinkering back in my own kitchen (and many phone calls with Obā-chan) to get them right.

In all my years of saying *no, thank you* to bowls of udon noodle soup and sweet red bean soup with mochi, I came to realize how distant I had started to feel from my family and my culture, too. Food is an essential form of communication for many Asian families, and my eating disorder kept closing that door. While trying to master Obā-chan's recipes, I spent more time with her than I had since our first move to Taiwan, making up for earlier years. I'd hover over the stove with her, asking questions about the different variations of recipes based on region in Japan.

So as it turns out, rice is not the enemy, and my dad was right about the best white rice being made in a rice cooker, though Obā-chan might argue with him over whether or not you should wash the rice first.

thai basil tempeh

Pad gra prow, or Thai basil beef, is a staple dish that you'll find on menus all over Thailand. On one of our first trips to Thailand, this dish became my dad's go-to order for nearly every single meal. Now his favorite place to get pad gra prow is, surprisingly, at a cheap mini restaurant inside a local Thai grocery store chain, Foodland. It's an unassuming, homey dish and, according to Dad, it's (unsurprisingly!) best prepared simply, no frills, as it is intended to be eaten. This rendition has all the flavors of pad gra pow but with tempeh, a meaty substitute for the beef.

MAKES 3 TO 4 SERVINGS

8 ounces tempeh

2 small Thai red chilis, thinly sliced (more or less, to taste)

2 garlic cloves, minced

2 tablespoons neutral oil (see page xvi)

One 4-inch red spur chili, thinly sliced

1 tablespoon tamari

1 teaspoon coconut sugar

1 teaspoon gluten-free vegetarian oyster sauce

1 cup Thai basil (or holy basil) leaves

Cooked jasmine rice, for serving

1. Start by preparing the tempeh: Crumble it with your hands or quickly pulse in a food processor until it resembles the texture of ground beef.

2. Using a mortar and pestle, smash the Thai red chilis and garlic to form a paste. Alternatively, you can finely mince with a knife, with a back-and-forth rocking movement, until nicely broken down.

3. In a wok or large frying pan, heat the oil over medium heat. Add the chili-garlic paste and sauté for 2 to 3 minutes, until nice and aromatic. Add the tempeh and cook for 2 to 3 minutes, until the paste has coated the tempeh, then add the red spur chili, soy sauce, coconut sugar, and oyster sauce. Toss to coat evenly. Cook for 2 minutes, until the sauce has mostly been absorbed by the tempeh.

4. Add the basil and turn off the heat. Toss to incorporate and serve with jasmine rice.

coconut lime rice

Many people think of rice as bland, but it's so fragrant, especially when prepared correctly. Add aromatics, fat, and acid and the humble grain is completely transformed. This coconut lime rice is fluffy, buttery, and zingy and the perfect complement to many main dishes.

MAKES 3 TO 4 SERVINGS

1 cup uncooked basmati or jasmine rice

1 tablespoon vegan butter, optional

1 cup full-fat coconut milk

1 cup filtered water

2 tablespoons freshly squeezed lime juice

2 or 3 lime leaves (fresh, frozen, or dried), optional

1 or 2 pandan leaves (fresh, frozen, or dried), optional

Pinch of kosher salt

Grated fresh lime zest, for garnish

1. Wash the rice thoroughly by rinsing it in a fine-mesh strainer or colander, then drain.

2. In a small saucepan over medium heat, melt the vegan butter, if using, and toast the rice for 3 to 4 minutes, until it is glossy and fragrant. Alternatively, dry toast the rice for 3 to 4 minutes until fragrant.

3. Add the coconut milk, water, lime juice, lime and pandan leaves, if using, and salt. Stir well and bring the mixture to a low boil, then reduce to a simmer and cover the pan. Cook for about 20 minutes, stirring occasionally, until all the liquid has been absorbed.

4. Remove from the heat, fluff with a fork, and garnish with lime zest. Toss to combine and enjoy.

oncle's onion pizza

Before Uncle Eugene opened his restaurants Cherry and Cherry Izakaya, my French uncle Raba had a restaurant called SoHo Steak. I was about five or six years old, still in my picky buttered noodle phase, and refused to eat anything from the menu. So Raba made me off-menu chicken noodle soup with his special addition of corn. Raba, like my Asian family, really connects with others through food. He can (and will) make conversation with just about anybody and everybody, but one thing I love about him is the way he'll offer food to others. In passing, he might offer you a small licorice pastille, his favorite candy from childhood, or a Ricola drop from his gingham shirt pocket, in case your throat feels hoarse. If you make a stop at the apartment he shares with Ohmi, he might offer you a little Trader Joe's dark chocolate with a handful of nuts.

If I had to pick one food that reminds me of Raba the most, though, it would have to be his onion pizza. No matter what else we're eating, you can rest assured that there will be a side of Raba's onion pizza. He makes his crust with pre-made dough from Trader Joe's—the best and most convenient crust you can get, he says. It's topped with anchovies and red onions before heading into the countertop toaster oven.

This pizza is Raba-inspired, but a little different; Raba doesn't measure his ingredients, and of course mine is vegan and gluten-free. It's a wonderful pizza to accompany any meal or can be enjoyed as a meal itself.

MAKES 1 PIZZA, TO SERVE 4 TO 5

Pictured on page 169

2 to 3 tablespoons olive oil, plus more as needed

2 white onions, thinly sliced

1 teaspoon kosher salt, plus more to taste

Gluten-Free Pizza Dough (page 178), parbaked (through step 4)

Vegan Ricotta Cheese (page 179), to taste

½ teaspoon red chili flakes

Freshly ground black pepper, to taste

1. Preheat the oven to 425°F.

2. In a heavy pan or Dutch oven, heat the olive oil over medium heat. Add the onions and toss to coat in oil. Cook for 8 to 10 minutes, stirring occasionally, until tender, then add the salt. Continue to cook for 30 to 40 minutes, until the onions are a deep brown. Be careful not to stir the onions too much; let them brown until they slightly stick to the pan, and then stir to release. Set aside.

3. Brush the parbaked pizza dough with olive oil. Spread the caramelized onions over the crust and dollop the vegan ricotta all over. Sprinkle with the red chili flakes and drizzle with olive oil. Bake for 5 to 8 minutes, until the crust is lightly golden brown. Finish with salt and pepper as desired, cut up the pizza, and serve.

more things my family members, who never measure anything, like to make

gluten-free pizza dough

Here's a simple pizza crust recipe that comes together in one bowl. The dough does not rise very much (thanks to the gluten-free flour blend), but I still like adding yeast for the flavor.

MAKES 1 MEDIUM PIZZA CRUST

2 teaspoons instant yeast

1 teaspoon coconut sugar

¾ cup plus 1 tablespoon warm (around 110°F) water

1¾ cups gluten-free flour (see page xv)

2 tablespoons neutral oil (see page xvi), plus more as needed

½ teaspoon kosher salt

Toppings of your choice

1. In the bowl of a stand mixer with a paddle attachment, combine the yeast, coconut sugar, and warm water. Let sit for about 5 minutes to activate the yeast; it should be slightly bubbly and frothy.

2. Add the flour, oil, and salt and mix until a workable dough ball forms. Coat the dough ball with oil and transfer to a bowl and cover with a damp cloth to rest for about 1 hour.

3. To parbake the crust, preheat the oven to 425°F and line a metal pizza pan or half-sheet pan with parchment paper or a nonstick baking mat.

4. Set the dough on the prepared pan. Use greased hands to gently press the dough down until the pan is evenly covered. Use a fork to dock the crust and create steam holes all over, as you would a pie crust. Parbake for 8 to 10 minutes, until lightly golden.

5. To finish the pizza: Add the toppings of your choice and bake the pizza until the toppings are nicely cooked and the crust is golden, 5 to 6 minutes (the cooking time will vary depending on the toppings).

vegan ricotta cheese

This is one of my favorite vegan cheeses to make because it's so easy and uses a base of tofu. It can be enjoyed with pasta and pizza, on toast, and more.

MAKES 5 TO 6 SERVINGS

3 tablespoons nutritional yeast

5 garlic cloves, peeled

2 tablespoons extra virgin olive oil

1 tablespoon white miso paste

Juice of ½ lemon

1 teaspoon kosher salt, plus more to taste

½ teaspoon freshly ground black pepper, plus more to taste

One 15-ounce package firm tofu

Combine the nutritional yeast, garlic, olive oil, miso paste, lemon juice, salt, and pepper in a blender or food processor. Give the mixture a rough pulse to break down the garlic slightly. Press the tofu between two kitchen linens with your hands to remove excess water, then place it in the food processor and pulse again until the mixture is evenly combined and has taken on the texture of ricotta. The result should be slightly chunky, not completely smooth, but you can adjust the texture to your preference. Season with more salt and pepper if needed. The ricotta can be stored in an airtight container in the refrigerator for up to a week.

popcorn tofu

Every afternoon in elementary school, I'd leave the Taipei American School gates and instantly be greeted by the smell of Taiwanese popcorn chicken. This tofu version makes the kitchen smell just like Taipei.

MAKES 4 SERVINGS

¼ cup plus 1 tablespoon neutral oil (see page xvi)

7 or 8 Thai basil leaves

One 15-ounce package extra-firm tofu

¼ cup cornstarch (see Note)

2 garlic cloves, crushed

1½ teaspoons tamari

2 teaspoons toasted sesame oil

2 teaspoons five-spice powder

1 teaspoon organic cane sugar

½ teaspoon kosher salt

½ teaspoon ground white pepper

SEASONING MIX

½ teaspoon five-spice powder

½ teaspoon mushroom powder (see page xvi)

½ teaspoon kosher salt

½ teaspoon freshly ground black pepper

½ teaspoon ground white pepper

1. Preheat the oven to 400°F.

2. In a small pot or shallow pan, off heat, combine ¼ cup of the neutral oil and the basil leaves. Turn the heat to medium and bring to a sizzle. Let cook for 1 to 2 minutes, stirring constantly, until the basil starts to shrivel. Remove the basil from the oil and set aside on a paper towel.

3. To prepare the tofu, press it between two kitchen linens with your hands to remove excess water. Use your hands to tear the tofu into chunks that resemble chicken nuggets. In a medium shallow bowl, toss the tofu in the cornstarch to coat. Arrange the tofu on a sheet pan (don't crowd the pieces too much) and bake for 10 minutes, until lightly golden.

4. In a medium bowl, mix the remaining 1 tablespoon oil with the garlic, soy sauce, sesame oil, five-spice, sugar, salt, and white pepper. Toss the tofu in the mixture, spread it across the sheet pan again, and bake for 12 to 15 minutes, until crisp.

5. Meanwhile, to prepare the seasoning mix, combine all the ingredients in a small bowl.

6. Toss the tofu and basil leaves in a large bowl to combine. To finish, add the seasoning mix and toss until evenly coated. Enjoy hot!

NOTE: *For better crunch, use 2 tablespoons cornstarch plus 2 tablespoons potato starch in place of the ¼ cup cornstarch. It's an extra ingredient, but it makes a difference in the final result!*

two-minute tofu

This dish is almost as easy to put together as a bowl of cereal. Next time you're in a pinch, or want to make a quick appetizer, this is the recipe! Serve it cold, or if you prefer it hot, steam it in a steamer basket over medium heat until hot to the touch.

MAKES 2 TO 3 SERVINGS

One 15-ounce package silken tofu, drained

2 tablespoons Everything Bagel Chili Crisp (page 192)

1 tablespoon tamari

2 teaspoons gluten-free vegetarian mushroom oyster sauce

1 teaspoon organic cane sugar

1 teaspoon toasted sesame oil

2 scallions, thinly sliced

Flaky salt, to taste

1. Drain the tofu in its package, flip the container over onto a plate or flat bowl, and remove the container.

2. In a small bowl, mix together the chili crisp, tamari, mushroom oyster sauce, sugar, and sesame oil. Pour it over the tofu. Garnish with sliced scallions and flaky salt and enjoy cold.

dad's crunchy potatoes

I'm a bad Korean. I don't like kimchi, which means a lot of Korean dishes are off the table for me, literally and figuratively. Anytime I eat with my dad's side of the family, they offer me kimchi in the hope that maybe one day I'll outgrow my "phase" and perhaps become a little more Korean in the process. It's choreography at this point—the kimchi is passed around, my halmoni offers it to me, and after twenty-nine years she is still surprised when I turn down the offer. We all laugh about it—until the next meal.

My dad likes to say he doesn't really care for food the way Mom's side of the family does. He once told me that it was tough to date my mom when they were growing up because her favorite foods weren't "real food" to him. Pizza, sandwiches, and Spanish tapas were things my dad *learned* to enjoy, but if it was up to him, he'd keep it simple. Steamed short-grain white rice, properly cooked in a Korean singing rice cooker; simple raw vegetables like peppers, perilla leaves, lettuce, cucumbers; and sides of kimchi, pickled Korean ingredients, and *ssamjang* (red pepper paste). Simple. When he's feeling sick, it's a simple bowl of leftover rice, lots of hot water, and kimchi. A lazy porridge, if you will. It's true that Dad eats simply and never really gets too excited about dinner, or about trying new foods when we travel—with the exception of Korean food itself. If he's choosing where we eat out, it's Korean. And there's nothing more he loves to make for my sisters and me than Korean food, even if it's an instant ramen pack.

After my first semester of college and my foray into veganism, I came home for winter break. We went to our usual Korean spot as a family, and I remember my dad's disappointment when I told him that I might eat ahead of time, in case I couldn't find anything I could have. I brought an emergency snack with me but settled on the dolsot bibimbap (no egg, no meat), and this became my standard order every time we ate out at Korean restaurants. Eventually I grew tired of eating the same dish over and over. I said something along the lines of, "I don't want Korean food anymore," and Dad looked crestfallen, as if I'd actually said, "I don't want to be Korean anymore."

Later that week, Dad excitedly brought me a thick, glossy cookbook written in Korean, which I could sound out, but not necessarily understand. It was temple food, my dad explained, which meant it was all vegan—but still Korean. We flipped through the pages together, as he dog-eared recipes he thought I should try out. We started experimenting with traditional dishes

we loved, like *doenjang jjigae*, a spicy fermented soybean stew, and labored together over *jjajangmyeon*, black bean paste noodles.

My dad may think that food isn't as important to him as it is to other people, but he shows us otherwise by sharing Korean cuisine with us and taking pride when we enjoy kimbap or appreciate his perfectly cooked rice. It's why he went to lengths to try to introduce Korean dishes to my vegan culinary vocabulary, ordered special Korean ingredients free of animal products online, and always made sure I wasn't going hungry. It's why he decided that he, too, should try out a vegan diet for a bit, so he could eat with me. I often made my own side of food that was either a vegan version of our family meal or something different altogether, and for about a year, I cooked for two.

When I served Dad black bean burgers or shared my latest take on a meatless "chicken nugget" with him, I understood why our family dinners at Korean restaurants were so meaningful.

The first time I ate his crunchy potatoes, I thought he had undercooked them. But Dad says it's the only way he likes to eat potatoes, and I learned to enjoy them in a completely different way! In his style, of course, the recipe is extremely simple. The potatoes can be served on their own or with a side of rice.

MAKES 3 TO 4 SERVINGS

2 tablespoons neutral oil (see page xvi)

4 garlic cloves, crushed

2 scallions, white parts thinly sliced, green parts sliced diagonally

½ white onion, thinly sliced

2 or 3 medium yellow potatoes (see Note), peeled and sliced into sticks about the thickness of chopsticks

1 teaspoon kosher salt, plus more to taste

Tamari

Ground white pepper

1. Heat the oil in a large pan over medium heat. Add the garlic and cook for about a minute, until fragrant. Add the scallion white parts and the onion and sauté for 1 to 2 minutes, until fragrant and slightly tender.

2. Add the potato sticks and sauté for about 5 minutes; the potatoes should still have some crunch to them, with not too much color or browning.

3. Season with the salt. Add tamari and white pepper to taste and toss to evenly distribute. Garnish with the green parts of the scallions and serve.

NOTE: *In Shanghai, where Dad now lives, the potato availability is not so diverse; do your best to find a smooth, thin-skinned potato about the size of a fist and a half.*

fridge cleanout veggie pancakes

Whenever my family eats at a Korean restaurant, the *pajeon*, or Korean pancake, is one of the most highly anticipated dishes. Though not the main event, it's one of those menu items that everyone at the table enjoys, and it's also really easy to make at home. Usually, it's a fritter-like pancake chock-full of vegetables and seafood, but it's equally good with just vegetables. I like to use veggies in season and switch them up every time, though sometimes I'll let the fridge leftovers decide for me. Use whatever you like—just make sure you end up with about 5 cups of vegetable filling. Aside from the veggies, you'll need only a few extra ingredients, so this is also an excellent dish to make when you're asking yourself what to make for dinner. Don't be shy with the oil—you'll want crispy edges all around!

MAKES 5 TO 6 PANCAKES

1¼ cups gluten-free flour (see page xv)

¼ cup cornstarch

1 teaspoon baking powder

Pinch of kosher salt, plus more to taste

1¼ cups warm water

½ yellow onion, thinly sliced

3 scallions, thinly sliced

2 zucchini, halved lengthwise and cut into thin half-moons

2 carrots, peeled and julienned

¾ cup thinly sliced cabbage

Neutral oil (see page xvi)

Tamari Vinaigrette (page 79), or the dipping sauce of your choice

1. In a large bowl, whisk together the flour, cornstarch, baking powder, and salt, then slowly pour in the warm water while you continue to whisk to create the batter.

2. Add all the vegetables to the batter and toss to combine. The mixture will be more veggies than batter.

3. Bring a large skillet or frying pan up to medium-high heat and coat it with a generous amount of oil. Ladle in a scoop of the batter, about ¼ cup, then use chopsticks or the back of the ladle to spread the batter as thin as you can. The thinner the better! Cook, turning once, until golden brown on both sides, 5 to 7 minutes per side. Season with salt, then remove the pancakes from the pan and let cool on a wire rack. Repeat with the remaining batter.

4. Enjoy with Tamari Vinaigrette or another dipping sauce.

spicy scalloped potatoes

Potatoes are a crowd pleaser, and there are a million ways to enjoy them! This dish is a vegan take on scalloped potatoes or gratin, but with a creamy and spicy gochujang sauce. It's irresistible and perfect for a cozy dinner or family meal.

MAKES 8 TO 10 SERVINGS

⅔ cup raw cashews, soaked in water overnight or boiled for 5 minutes, then drained

1⅔ cups unsweetened plant milk of your choice

1¼ cups water or vegetable broth

1 tablespoon olive oil

¼ cup nutritional yeast

3 tablespoons gochujang

2 teaspoons mushroom powder (see page xvi)

2 teaspoons garlic powder

1 teaspoon onion powder

2 teaspoons kosher salt, plus more as needed

2½ pounds russet potatoes

Freshly ground black pepper, to taste

4 scallions, green parts only, thinly sliced

1 tablespoon vegan butter, optional

1. Preheat the oven to 350°F.

2. To make the sauce, place the cashews, plant milk, water, olive oil, nutritional yeast, gochujang, mushroom powder, garlic powder, onion powder, and salt in a high-powered blender and blend until completely smooth. Adjust the seasoning to your taste. Be generous with the salt if the mixture feels flat; it helps to bring out the flavors. Set the sauce aside.

3. Peel the potatoes, if desired (I like to keep the skin on), and slice a small piece off the top of each one to create a flat surface. Using a mandoline, slice the potatoes very thinly. They should be thin but still hold their shape.

4. Pour one-fourth of the sauce into the bottom of a 9 x 13-inch baking dish and gently arrange one-third of the potatoes, overlapping slightly, to cover the bottom of the dish. Cover the potatoes with one-third of the remaining sauce and sprinkle a handful of scallions on top. Lay half of the remaining potatoes on top. Cover the potatoes with half of the remaining sauce, then the rest of the potatoes and the rest of the sauce. Sprinkle on the remaining scallions.

5. Cover with foil and bake for 45 minutes. Remove the foil and bake for another 15 minutes, until the potatoes are fork tender.

6. If using, cut the vegan butter into small pieces and spread them across the surface of the potatoes. Broil for 2 to 3 minutes for a nice golden top. Season with a touch of salt and the pepper, then serve.

everything bagel chili crisp

Classic chili crisp meets everything bagel flavor in this fun and versatile condiment—and it will make the kitchen smell incredible. Do be careful working with hot oil and be sure that all the containers you're using are heat-safe. And feel free to customize the crisp to your liking! I use this in any recipe that calls for chili crisp, such as Cucumber Sesame Noodles (page 146).

MAKES ABOUT 1 CUP

1 tablespoon black sesame seeds

1 tablespoon white sesame seeds

⅔ cup neutral oil (see page xvi)

1 shallot, thinly sliced

3 garlic cloves, thinly sliced

2 tablespoons poppy seeds

2 tablespoons gochugaru

2 tablespoons Aleppo pepper flakes

2 garlic cloves, minced

2 teaspoons flaky salt, plus more to taste

½ teaspoon toasted sesame oil, plus more to taste

1. In a small dry skillet over medium-high heat, toast the black and white sesame seeds for 2 to 3 minutes, shaking frequently, until golden and aromatic (take care not to burn them). Remove from the heat and set aside.

2. Off the heat, pour the oil into a small saucepan and add the shallot. Place the pan over medium-low heat, bring the shallot to a nice sizzle, and cook, stirring frequently, until it starts to turn a golden-brown color, 15 to 20 minutes. Use a slotted spoon to remove the shallot to a paper towel–lined tray.

3. Strain the oil to remove any remaining sediment, then return it to the saucepan. Add the thinly sliced garlic and cook over medium-low heat and, again, wait for a nice sizzle. Cook, stirring constantly to avoid burning, until a golden-brown color, about 5 minutes. Transfer to the paper towel–lined tray. Strain the oil again and return it to the saucepan.

4. Heat the oil to 225°F to 245°F. (It's best to use a thermometer if you have one, but if not, test the temperature by dropping in a small piece of vegetable trim, or a sesame seed, to see if it fries up on contact.)

5. While the oil is heating, in a large, heat-safe bowl, combine the toasted sesame seeds with the poppy seeds, gochugaru, Aleppo pepper flakes, minced garlic, and salt.

6. Carefully pour the hot oil over the ingredients in the bowl. Everything should start to sizzle and bubble. When the bubbling slows, stir to make sure all the ingredients hit the oil. Let sit for 20 to 30 minutes to infuse and cool completely.

7. Gently crush the fried sliced garlic and shallot with your palm or a knife. Add both to the cooled chili oil and stir to combine. Taste and add more salt if you like. Let cool completely and store in an airtight container in the refrigerator for up to 1 month.

7 you deserve it

One of the most memorable Manhattan moments of my life is the day I walked to Levain Bakery with a friend from my college French class. It happened to be blizzarding that day, but nearly all the cafés and bakeries were still brewing coffee and baking bread: It was business as usual, and I'd expect nothing less in Manhattan. Levain Bakery is one of the city's hot spots—a must for tourists but also frequented by locals. Even outside of New York, their fist-size, ooey-gooey chocolate chip cookies are famous. Up until that snowy day, even after all my years of living in New York, I had yet to try one. I would tell my therapist later how I ate the cookie warm and enjoyed the crispy edges and near-underbaked interior equally, and how I struggled to wipe the melted chocolate off my face and how I couldn't stop at just half, like I had intended to. While waiting in line, someone cracked a joke about the cookies being calorically dense enough to be their entire intake for the day, and that thought crossed my mind as I finished the cookie. I was proud, oddly, that I had eaten the whole thing and for once had not spent time on Google and MyFitnessPal, trying to figure out how many calories were *really* in it. Truth be told, putting my shoes on to walk to the cafeteria for dinner that night was challenging. I didn't feel like I deserved to eat any more for the day, knowing how dense that Levain cookie was. It even had walnuts, I told myself, a high-calorie, rich, and buttery ingredient. I opted for a salad even though the mac and cheese looked delicious, but eating dinner at all was a feat at that time.

Something about chocolate chip cookies was always irresistible, even in my darkest days, when my fear of food was at an all-time high. I wouldn't eat avocados because I had decided that they were pure fat and calories, but a chocolate chip cookie? I'd never say no. Food is fuel and nutrition is important, but sometimes food is comfort. Chocolate chip cookies were pure comfort for me for many, many years. They quelled my hunger pangs in middle school and were a food I knew I could always reliably eat, even on days when food was my enemy. I owe a lot to chocolate chip cookies for holding my hand and teaching me that no matter what, we all deserve to eat and dessert is not something to be earned.

In Asian culture, it's common to compliment a dessert by saying it's "not too sweet." Asian desserts are often mildly sweet compared to American ones. For example, *zenzai*, the Japanese red bean soup, has an earthy flavor and its main ingredient is often consumed in savory dishes in other countries. *It's* often served alongside a cup of hot, astringent tea, for balance.

Because I grew up eating zenzai and kinako for dessert, balance is something I value in the dessert recipes I create. Still, my favorite way to create is to experiment with mash-ups of American desserts and Asian flavors. With a little bit of matcha and miso paste, these are desserts that will satisfy your sweet tooth while also earning Obā-chan's nod of approval.

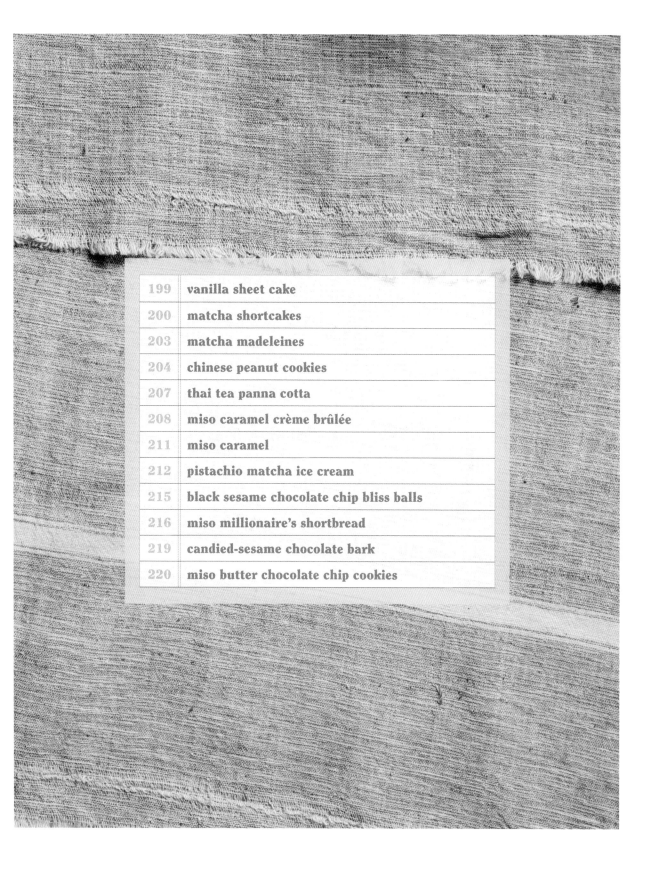

vanilla sheet cake

I always looked forward to school functions and in-class birthdays, just because I loved grocery store sheet cakes. This simple vanilla sheet cake is reminiscent of that unassuming sponge cake base and can be frosted flat, stacked into a tiered cake, used to make shortcakes, and more. Top with fresh fruit, roughly chopped nuts, sprinkles, toasted coconut flakes, or anything else your heart desires.

MAKES 1 SHEET CAKE

Cooking spray or vegan butter

1½ cups plant milk of your choice

1 tablespoon apple cider vinegar

3 cups gluten-free flour (see page xv)

2 teaspoons baking powder

1 teaspoon baking soda

1½ cups organic cane sugar

1 cup (2 sticks) vegan butter, softened

¾ cup unsweetened applesauce

1 teaspoon vanilla bean paste or pure vanilla extract

1. Preheat the oven to 350°F. Grease a full sheet pan with cooking spray.

2. Combine the plant milk and vinegar in a medium bowl and let sit for 10 minutes to create a vegan buttermilk.

3. In a large bowl, whisk together the flour, baking powder, baking soda, and sugar. Add the plant milk mixture, butter, applesauce, and vanilla. Stir until a smooth batter forms.

4. Pour the batter into the prepared sheet pan, spreading it out evenly with a spatula. Bake for 35 to 40 minutes, until the cake pulls away from the sides of the pan and a toothpick inserted in the center comes out clean.

5. Let cool completely before frosting or adding any toppings, cutting, and serving. Store leftovers in the refrigerator in an airtight container for up to 1 week.

matcha shortcakes

This is the perfect dessert to enjoy alongside a cup of tea or hot matcha. I love the combination of bright green matcha cream piled on top of springy vanilla sheet cake rounds and fresh strawberries. The earthiness of the matcha helps balance the sweetness of this classic dessert and adds a little something extra fun.

MAKES 4 TO 5 SHORTCAKES

Vanilla Sheet Cake (page 199)

One 14-ounce can coconut cream, refrigerated for at least 3 hours or overnight

½ cup powdered sugar

1½ teaspoons vanilla bean paste

1 teaspoon ceremonial-grade matcha powder, sifted, plus more for garnish

¼ teaspoon kosher salt

1 cup sliced fresh strawberries

1. Use a 4-inch cookie cutter or upside-down glass to cut an even number of rounds out of the sheet cake. Set aside.

2. In a stand mixer fitted with a whisk attachment, whip the coconut cream, powdered sugar, vanilla bean paste, sifted matcha powder, and salt until fluffy enough to resemble whipped cream.

3. To assemble each shortcake, spoon about ¼ cup matcha cream on top of one cake round. Top with strawberries, pressing them into the cream. Add another cake round and top with cream again. Decorate with more strawberries and, if desired, dust with matcha powder.

matcha madeleines

My earliest baking memories are all at my aunt Ohmi's apartment in Manhattan. We'd make Oreo cheesecake from a Jell-O dessert kit, or a pan of her favorite madeleines. I remember wanting to drink the bottle of vanilla extract because it smelled so good, only to learn that it tasted awful by the spoonful. I found lemon zest to be a little too bitter for my four-year-old palate, so we'd make one batch of madeleines with and one without. These days, I prefer them flavored with matcha. I always think of her when I see a madeleine or financier, and this matcha madeleine takes me back to her kitchen.

If you don't have a madeleine pan, you can use a mini muffin pan instead.

MAKES 12 MADELEINES

Cooking spray

½ cup powdered sugar

3 to 4 teaspoons ceremonial-grade matcha powder

1 cup gluten-free flour (see page xv)

1 teaspoon baking powder

1 cup soymilk, homemade (page 116) or store-bought (or the plant milk of your choice)

3 tablespoons neutral oil (see page xvi)

1 teaspoon pure vanilla extract

½ teaspoon kosher salt

1. Preheat the oven to 350°F and spray a madeleine pan with cooking spray.

2. Whisk together the powdered sugar and 2 teaspoons of the matcha powder in a small bowl and set aside.

3. In a large bowl, combine the flour and baking powder and whisk well. Add the soymilk, oil, vanilla, salt, and 1 to 2 teaspoons of the remaining matcha powder (add more for a stronger matcha flavor and less if you prefer it mild) and whisk until combined. Scoop the batter into the prepared pan, about 1½ tablespoons batter per mold. Spread out the batter; it will not spread on its own in the oven.

4. Bake for 10 minutes, or until a toothpick inserted in the center of a madeleine comes out clean. Let the madeleines rest in the pan until cool, then dust with the matcha powdered sugar.

chinese peanut cookies

Chinese peanut cookies are a classic dessert that melt in your mouth, similar to snowball cookies. They are full of peanut flavor, rich, and buttery—and are really easy to make with only five ingredients. And, most important, they're not too sweet. They are commonly enjoyed to celebrate Chinese New Year, but I think they deserve to be shared year-round: They're that good!

This recipe calls for optional aquafaba, the liquid from a can of chickpeas that can be used as substitute for egg whites. It contributes the same glossy effect as egg whites when brushed over the cookies before baking.

MAKES 12 COOKIES

1½ cups roasted peanuts, pulsed in the food processor to form a fine powder

1 cup gluten-free flour (see page xv), plus more as needed

½ cup powdered sugar

½ cup peanut oil

2 tablespoons unsweetened creamy peanut butter

Aquafaba, for glazing, optional

1. In a large bowl, whisk together the ground peanuts, flour, and powdered sugar. Add the peanut oil and peanut butter and mix until well incorporated and a workable dough forms. If the mixture is too moist to handle, add up to ¼ cup more flour until the right texture is achieved. Cover the dough and chill in the refrigerator for at least 30 minutes, or up to an hour.

2. Preheat the oven to 350°F and line a sheet pan with parchment paper or a nonstick baking mat.

3. Roll 1½-tablespoon portions of the dough into 12 balls and place on the prepared sheet pan, leaving 1½ inches between each. Brush the cookies with aquafaba, if desired.

4. Bake for 18 minutes, until golden brown. They won't expand much. Let cool completely before handling! Store in an airtight container at room temperature for up to 1 week.

thai tea panna cotta

You can make this dairy-free, tea-infused panna cotta in minutes! And it's a great dessert for entertaining because it's easy to prepare in large batches. If Thai tea isn't your thing, try another loose-leaf tea in its place and enjoy! Serve with fruit, plant-based whipped cream, and any other desired toppings.

MAKES 2 SERVINGS

1½ cups unsweetened oat milk

1 tablespoon Thai tea leaves

1 tablespoon pure maple syrup

1 teaspoon agar agar powder (see page xiii)

1 teaspoon vanilla bean paste

Pinch of kosher salt

1. In a small pot over low heat, bring the milk and tea leaves to a low boil. Lower the heat to a simmer and cook for 3 minutes to begin the steeping process. Set aside off the heat to steep for 30 minutes. Strain out the tea leaves and return the tea to the pot.

2. Bring the tea to a low simmer over medium-low heat, then add the maple syrup, agar agar powder, vanilla bean paste, and salt. Cook, whisking continuously, for 3 minutes to activate the agar.

3. Divide the mixture between two 6-ounce ramekins and chill for 3 hours, or overnight.

4. To serve, gently invert the panna cotta onto a small plate (it should come out quite easily) or enjoy it right from the ramekin.

miso caramel crème brûlée

When I was a kid, Uncle Raba loved to make crème brûlée—the classic dessert found at any French bistro—for me at his restaurant, SoHo Steak. Watching the sugar caramelize under the torch was fascinating to me, but I didn't learn to appreciate the "burnt" flavor until I was much older.

Of course, traditional crème brûlée is made with eggs and cream and thus isn't vegan. My version is made with a base of silken tofu and agar agar (which I like to call vegan gelatin). Below the classic caramelized sugar crust is a layer of miso caramel, a take on salted caramel but with extra depth of flavor. If you have yet to try miso in a dessert, fear not—I promise it's delicious.

MAKES 4 SERVINGS

12 ounces extra-firm silken tofu

⅔ cup unsweetened plant milk of your choice

¼ cup organic cane sugar, plus more for caramelizing

1 tablespoon unsweetened creamy cashew butter

2 teaspoons pure vanilla extract

1½ teaspoons agar agar powder (see page xiii)

½ teaspoon kosher salt

2 tablespoons Miso Caramel (page 211)

1. Combine the tofu, plant milk, sugar, cashew butter, vanilla, agar agar powder, and salt in a food processor or blender and process until completely smooth.

2. Transfer the mixture to a small saucepan and set over low heat. Cook for a few minutes, whisking constantly, until the mixture starts to thicken slightly. Set aside off the heat.

3. Spoon a thin layer of miso caramel into the bottom of four 6-ounce ramekins. Pour the agar agar mixture into the ramekins and chill in the fridge until set, at least 3 hours. The mixture should firm up considerably.

4. When ready to serve, sprinkle the tops with additional sugar (about 1 teaspoon per ramekin, more as needed), then use a kitchen blowtorch to caramelize the sugar. The sugar will bubble, brown, and turn an amber color when ready. Let cool to harden, then enjoy!

miso caramel

This miso caramel is made from Medjool dates instead of refined sugar and resembles salted caramel with an even deeper umami flavor. It's fantastic on top of ice cream, can be warmed up to enjoy with baked goods, and can even be blended into smoothies and other drinks to add that salted caramel flavor. P.S.: No stove is required!

MAKES ABOUT 1 CUP

1 cup Medjool dates (about 12 dates), pitted

¼ cup plant milk of your choice, plus more as needed

1½ teaspoons vanilla bean paste or pure vanilla extract

¼ cup unsweetened cashew butter (or coconut cream, to make the caramel nut-free)

2 tablespoons white miso paste, plus more to taste

1. If the dates feel dry and hard to the touch, soak them in hot water for 10 minutes before blending, making sure to drain off any excess water. Blend the dates with the plant milk and vanilla in a high-powered blender until a smooth paste forms.

2. Add the cashew butter and miso paste and blend until smooth. Add more plant milk as desired to adjust the texture. Taste and add more miso paste if you desire. Transfer to an airtight container to store in the refrigerator for up to a week.

pistachio matcha ice cream

My family home had pints of ice cream in the freezer at all times (courtesy of Raba, my French uncle). My pick was always pistachio. This no-churn ice cream is a beautiful shade of green and has a lovely creaminess coming from the roasted pistachios.

MAKES ABOUT 1 PINT

1 cup shelled roasted pistachios

1 cup unsweetened soymilk, homemade (page 116) or store-bought (or the plant milk of your choice)

3 to 4 tablespoons pure maple syrup, or to taste

2 teaspoons ceremonial-grade matcha powder

1½ teaspoons vanilla bean paste

½ teaspoon kosher salt

1. Soak the pistachios in hot water for 30 minutes to soften, then drain.

2. Combine ¾ cup of the pistachios with the soymilk, maple syrup, matcha powder, vanilla bean paste, and salt in a high-powered blender and blend until smooth. Strain for extra silkiness.

3. Mix in the remaining ¼ cup pistachios, then pour into a freezer-safe container, cover, and freeze until solid. Let thaw for 10 to 15 minutes, then scoop to serve.

SOFT SERVE PISTACHIO MATCHA ICE CREAM

For a soft serve–like texture, freeze the mixture in an ice cube tray without the whole pistachios. When the cubes are frozen, blend them in a high-powered blender, using a tamper to help break down the cubes, until smooth. Once blended, fold in the pistachios and enjoy immediately.

black sesame chocolate chip bliss balls

This dessert-snack hybrid takes no time at all to prepare and is a great on-the-go bite. It's full of flavor and texture and it's *not too sweet.*

1 cup raw cashews

½ teaspoon kosher salt

15 Medjool dates, pitted (if they aren't soft, soak them in hot water for 10 minutes, then drain)

2 tablespoons tahini, optional

1 teaspoon vanilla bean paste

1 tablespoon cacao powder

3 tablespoons dairy-free mini chocolate chips (I like the Enjoy Life brand)

2 tablespoons toasted black sesame seeds

1.   Combine the cashews and salt in a food processor and process until finely ground. Be sure not to overprocess or you'll end up with cashew butter. Add the dates, tahini, and vanilla bean paste and pulse until a dough forms. Add the cacao powder and pulse again. The mixture should start to pull away from the sides of the food processor and hold together with ease when squished between your fingers. Add the chocolate chips and sesame seeds and pulse a few times, just enough to incorporate into the dough.

2.   Roll the dough into balls using 1 or 2 tablespoons each and enjoy. Store in an airtight container in the refrigerator for up to 1 week or in the freezer for up to 2 months.

miso millionaire's shortbread

One restaurant that forever has a place in my heart is Slice in Shanghai. It's no longer open, but it was just a few blocks away from the last apartment we lived in before I left for college. My favorite menu item was their millionaire's shortbread. It was my first time ever having it and I loved the buttery shortbread base, gooey caramel, and chocolate top. This no-bake version is easy to make with whole food ingredients and is perfect to keep in the refrigerator to munch on whenever you're needing something sweet.

MAKES 10 SERVINGS

1 cup plus 2 tablespoons almond flour

Pinch of kosher salt

3 tablespoons pure maple syrup

3 tablespoons coconut oil, softened

Miso Caramel (page 211)

⅔ cup dairy-free dark chocolate chips (I like the Enjoy Life brand)

1. In a medium bowl, mix the almond flour, salt, maple syrup, and 2 tablespoons of the coconut oil until combined.

2. Line a 4 x 8-inch loaf pan with parchment paper, leaving some hanging over the long sides to make it easy to remove the dessert from the pan. Place the dough in the pan and press down to create an even shortbread crust. Smear an even layer of miso caramel over the shortbread.

3. Melt the chocolate chips with the remaining 1 tablespoon coconut oil in the microwave or a double boiler. Spread the melted chocolate evenly over the caramel layer. Refrigerate for at least 3 hours or overnight.

4. To serve, let sit at room temperature for 10 minutes, then remove the shortbread from the pan. Run a knife under hot water to warm it up before slicing the shortbread into 10 pieces, wiping the knife down and running it under hot water between slices. Store in the refrigerator for up to a week.

candied-sesame chocolate bark

This is one of my favorite confections to bring to family get-togethers because it's incredibly delicious but quicker to prepare than a baked good. Rich and silky chocolate gets a crumbled candied sesame topping that makes for a bite that's crunchy, nutty, buttery, salty, and sweet all at the same time.

MAKES 1 TRAY, FOR 6 TO 7 SERVINGS

3 tablespoons white sesame seeds

3 tablespoons black sesame seeds

¼ cup organic cane sugar

¼ cup filtered water

10 ounces dairy-free dark chocolate (I like the Enjoy Life brand), roughly chopped

Pinch flaky salt

1. Line two sheet pans with parchment paper or nonstick baking mats. Clear a space in the fridge for one of the sheet pans.

2. Toast all the sesame seeds in a small, dry skillet over low heat for 2 to 3 minutes, shaking frequently, until fragrant. Set aside.

3. Combine the sugar and filtered water in a small pot over medium-low heat. Heat, undisturbed, until the sugar dissolves and the mixture turns a light amber color and starts to bubble slightly, 4 to 5 minutes. Immediately add the toasted sesame seeds and begin stirring constantly until the sugar takes on a crumbly texture, 2 to 3 minutes. Remove from the heat and immediately transfer the mixture to one of the prepared sheet pans. Spread it out, breaking up any big clumps with a spatula, and let the candy cool completely.

4. Bring a small pot of tap water to a boil over medium-low heat. Place the chocolate in a medium, heat-safe bowl, set it on top of the pot, and stir constantly until melted. Alternatively, place the chocolate in a bowl and microwave in 15-second intervals, stirring in between, until melted.

5. Spread the chocolate evenly on the second prepared sheet pan. Sprinkle the sesame seed candy and flaky salt all over the chocolate. Transfer to the fridge to set. Once set, break up the bark into bite-size pieces. Store in an airtight container in a cool, dry place or the refrigerator for up to 2 weeks.

you deserve it

miso butter chocolate chip cookies

I will forever have a soft spot for chocolate chip cookies. They were my go-to afternoon snack most days in middle school, and to this day when I see a chocolate chip cookie on a dessert menu, I'll almost always order it. This version has a little extra depth of flavor thanks to miso butter, which adds umami, an unexpected sweetness, and savory notes.

MAKES ABOUT 12 COOKIES

8 tablespoons (1 stick) vegan butter, room temperature

¼ cup coconut sugar

¼ cup organic cane sugar

3 tablespoons white miso paste

3 tablespoons aquafaba (liquid from a can of chickpeas)

2 teaspoons pure vanilla extract

1¾ cups gluten-free flour (see page xv)

¼ teaspoon baking soda

¼ teaspoon baking powder

¾ cup dairy-free chocolate chips (I like the Enjoy Life brand)

1. In a medium bowl, whisk the butter, coconut sugar, cane sugar, and miso paste until smooth.

2. In a small bowl, vigorously whisk the aquafaba liquid until frothy. Add it to the butter mixture along with the vanilla and whisk to incorporate.

3. Sift in the flour, baking soda, and baking powder and stir using a spatula, just until the flour is incorporated and no dry clumps remain. Fold in the chocolate chips. Chill the dough, covered, for at least 1 hour, or up to overnight. This makes the dough easier to work with and reduces the amount of spreading in the oven.

4. Preheat the oven to 350°F. Line a sheet pan with parchment paper or a nonstick baking mat.

5. Use a cookie scoop to dollop the cookie dough onto the sheet, leaving 2 to 3 inches between each cookie to give them room. The cookies won't spread too much, so flatten them out just a bit using your hand.

6. Bake for 9 to 10 minutes, until the cookie edges are golden brown. If the center feels soft, be aware it will continue to set once out of the oven. Let cool completely and enjoy. Store leftovers in an airtight container in the fridge for up to a week.

acknowledgments

In 2018, I was invited to Gwyneth Paltrow's Goop Festival in New York City. There was a psychic on-site and the team booked me a session with her. I'd just quit my corporate job and had been sharing recipes on Instagram for a few years. The psychic told me that my calling in life was to write about food and that it would heal people. She also mentioned a significant date, which just so happened to be the date I'd put in my notice.

I didn't think too much about that encounter, but it was the first time I'd ever thought about writing a cookbook. I continued sharing recipes on Instagram and on my blog, and a year later, I received an e-mail from a publisher asking me if I had considered writing a cookbook. I thought it must be a sign from the universe and I put my all into writing a proposal with a complete recipe list. Progress was slow, for whatever reason, and then COVID-19 hit and I completely stopped work on the proposal.

Along with many other things in life, I continued to keep the cookbook on hold as I learned to navigate a post-COVID world. But in 2021, I reached out to a literary agent to help guide me as I worked toward wrapping up my proposal. Once again, progress was slow, but I felt strongly that the book needed to be written, and soon. My agent asked me to scratch numerous proposal ideas in favor of shifting to writing an Instant Pot cookbook, or one on the theme of hiding vegetables. My agent told me that there were already enough "ethnic" cookbooks out there and that she just "didn't get" the idea. Without that agent, I would not have fought as hard as I did for myself and my cookbook concept.

And so, I would like to start by thanking that first literary agent for showing me the ropes, teaching me how to write a proposal, and providing the fuel for my fire.

Brandon Skier, thank you for encouraging me to believe in the book, the endless feedback on recipes I was testing,

and introducing me to Anna Worrall, the literary agent responsible for pulling this dream out of the gutter and making it happen.

I am endlessly grateful to the William Morrow team, especially Cassie Jones and Jill Zimmerman, for seeing the vision and editing all my (many) British English spellings. I could not be more proud that my book found its home at HarperCollins.

A very special thanks to the team behind all the gorgeous photography—Kristin Teig, David Koung Peng, Marian Cairns, Alicia Buszczak, and Natalie Drobny. Every day on set was a party, and I loved eating Goop soup (with Justin Bieber playing softly in the background) with you all.

To Paulina Baray, who makes my life possible and kept me on track while testing recipes for this book, took home countless leftovers to share with her family for extra testing, and was my right-hand woman throughout this process, thank you.

To my family: In the process of writing this book, I found myself tapping into some of my core memories with you. Thank you for helping me become the person I am today, supporting my healing journey and transition to veganism (despite the initial skepticism), and passing down our culture and instilling it in me. Mum and Dad, I am eternally grateful that despite being Asian, you didn't get upset with me when I quit my corporate job to pursue "Instagram." Thank you for trying your best to transcribe our childhood recipes and picking up my countless FaceTime calls with food-related questions. Chloe and Avery, thank you for keeping me young and communicating with me via memes and TikTok videos. I love you, too. Ohmi, Raba, Eugene, and Roberta, I would not have survived my college years without you. Thank you for being my stand-in parents when my entire family was overseas. I always looked forward to weekends we'd spend together (and of course, all the food). Obā-chan and Jichang, I feel so lucky to have such supportive and inspiring grandparents. Thank you for cooking with me and for every sushi Saturday. Halmoni, thank you for

inspiring me as an artist with your creativity and giving Chloe, Avery, and me the gift of Korean home cooking.

To my friends, who kept me sane during some of my most trying times (including the ups and downs of writing the cookbook and an exploding oven), thank you from the bottom of my heart. Thank you for coming over to taste test recipes I was working on, taking leftovers home, checking in on me, and letting me run my short stories by you.

And finally, thank *you*. If you're reading this, thank you for giving me, and this book, a chance.

universal conversion chart

250°F = 120°C

275°F = 135°C

300°F = 150°C

325°F = 160°C

350°F = 180°C

375°F = 190°C

400°F = 200°C

425°F = 220°C

450°F = 230°C

475°F = 240°C

500°F = 260°C

MEASUREMENT EQUIVALENTS

Measurements should always be level unless directed otherwise.

⅛ teaspoon = 0.5 mL

¼ teaspoon = 1 mL

½ teaspoon = 2 mL

1 teaspoon = 5 mL

1 tablespoon = 3 teaspoons = ½ fluid ounce = 15 mL

2 tablespoons = ⅛ cup = 1 fluid ounce = 30 mL

4 tablespoons = ¼ cup = 2 fluid ounces = 60 mL

5⅓ tablespoons = ⅓ cup = 3 fluid ounces = 80 mL

8 tablespoons = ½ cup = 4 fluid ounces = 120 mL

10⅔ tablespoons = ⅔ cup = 5 fluid ounces = 160 mL

12 tablespoons = ¾ cup = 6 fluid ounces = 180 mL

16 tablespoons = 1 cup = 8 fluid ounces = 240 mL

index

NOTE: Page references in *italics* refer to photos.

index

HarperCollins books may be purchased for
educational, business, or sales promotional use.
For information, please email the Special Markets
Department at SPsales@harpercollins.com.

FIRST EDITION

DESIGNED BY RENATA DE OLIVEIRA
Photography by Kristin Teig

Library of Congress Cataloging-in-Publication
Data has been applied for.

ISBN 978-0-06-331102-2

24 25 26 27 28   IMG   10 9 8 7 6 5 4 3 2 1

REMY MORIMOTO PARK is a vegan and gluten-free recipe developer and health and wellness content creator. Originally from New Jersey, she has lived in New York, Shanghai, Taipei, and Bangkok and shares vibrant plant-based recipes, taking inspiration from her three cultures—Korean, Japanese, and Taiwanese—and all the countries she's lived in. She is a certified yoga and meditation teacher and holistic nutritionist, and her work has been featured by publications and outlets such as *Shape*, *British Vogue*, BuzzFeed, *Elle Vietnam*, CBS News, and ABC News. She lives in Los Angeles.

veggiekinsblog.com

B